TROTTER

PRESENTS

TREADMILL WALKING

A Motivational Resource for Treadmill Training

Robert Sweetgall

Edited by Robert Neeves, PhD

As You Begin Treadmill Walking

The motorized treadmill has become the most effective piece of fitness equipment for strengthening the heart, increasing endurance, burning fat, toning muscles, reducing stress, and improving mood and creativity – all in the boundaries of your home.

Training on a treadmill gives new energy to life. But success depends on working out consistently, with a purpose, and with a proper exercise prescription. That's why **Treadmill Walking** was written – to help you understand treadmill training and how to get the most for your money and your minute.

What follows is just about everything you'll ever need to know about treadmill training, including how to start a treadmill walking program; treadmill technique; assessing your aerobic capacity on a treadmill; progressing on a treadmill; walking for weight loss and cardiovascular endurance; and guidelines for purchasing a treadmill. In total over 25 creative workouts and training strategies are described and illustrated.

Many people who have never treadmilled think it's boring because of its repetitious nature. Others associate treadmilling with medical exams or cardiac rehab classes.

But for those who train on treadmills, the experience is beautifully simple, so natural, without hesitation, fear or pain. It frees the mind to travel where it has never gone before. A treadmill workout is a journey, a vacation from the nine-to-five race of making a living. It's your daily escape from the fast lane to some back-country roads where your creative mind can run wild.

To a great year of training and fantastic treadmill miles!

Rob Sweetgall,
President, Creative
Walking, Inc. and
Treadmill Consultant
to Trotter

Published by:
Creative Walking, Inc.
P.O. Box 699
Newark, DE 19711

Other books by Robert Sweetgall:
* **Fitness Walking**
* **Walking Wellness Student Workbook**
* **Walking Wellness Teacher's Guide**
* **The Walker's Journal**
* **Walking for Little Children**
* **Road Scholars**

Special Acknowledgements:
Peter Haines, Don Payne, Gordon Alling, Dave Clark, Jim Ahearn, Maryalyce
Deraad, Bill Domineau, Brian Lyman, Beth Russo, Roland Murray and the entire
Trotter support staff; John Aglialoro and Joan Carter of United Medical
Corporation; Dr. Robert Neeves; Dr. Stan Sady; Robert Pritikin, Dr. Tom
Anderson, Dave Liff, Marilyn Goldstein and The Pritikin Longevity Centers;
Drs. Barry and Sara Jane Bates; Al and Jan Norman; Lyvonne Crocco; Dottie
Magner, Micheal and Tracy Purdie; Paul, Mary and Kristen Krugreinhard; Pam
Berentsen; and Karen Ersek.

Cover Design: Lynne Tesch **Cover Photography:** Eric Crossan **Illustration and
Layout:** Gregory Stump, Karen Ersek, Lynne Tesch, Cindy Paige and Type
House of Iowa Inc. **On the Cover:** Lyvonne Crocco, Treadmill Walking 3.5 mph,
8% grade, 6 calories per minute.

A Word of Caution: Readers of **Treadmill Walking** should understand that there is
inherent risk in all types of exertional activities, whether it's physical labor at home or
work, high-intensity exercise, or treadmill walking and running. Furthermore, this risk
increases as we age and as certain lifestyle "risk factors" (such as high blood pressure,
cholesterol, sedentary living, obesity, smoking and family history) begin to develop in our
lives. If you are over 35 years, have any of these risk factors present in your life, or if you
suspect their presence or have a family history of heart disease, it is recommended that
you see your doctor, have a physical examination, and discuss the treadmill exercise program which is best for you **before** you start training.

In many cases, it is advisable to have a medically supervised treadmill tolerance test to
determine your maximum exertion level. Jim Fixx was advised to take such a test, but he
declined to do so. And like many who suffer heart attacks, he never got a second chance.

TABLE OF CONTENTS

Chapter 1

THE TREADMILL WALKING ADVANTAGE

Treadmilling – The Road To Lifelong Health.

Many people wonder, "Why train on a treadmill when you can simply walk outside?" This legitimate question deserves a legitimate answer. So here it is in a few words: *rain, snow, ice, traffic, dogs, potholes, pollution, security, convenience, efficiency, consistency* and *training capability.*

The fact is that quality motorized treadmills are the most effective fitness training devices in the world today. No other single piece of equipment can work as many large muscle groups naturally, without strain and discomfort.

The human body by itself cannot achieve the same training effect as the human body on a treadmill. Why? Because a treadmill keeps the body in motion. There's no "sluffing off" on a treadmill. The belt moves. You move.

*"All exercise equipment can be classified in two categories – **static** and **kinetic**. With static equipment, like bikes or rowers, you just sit there until you're ready to make it move. On a treadmill (kinetic), once you push the button, you have to keep up with it. It makes you go!"*

*Robert Jacobs
Treadmill Store Owner
The Walking Center*

Treadmills let you work against gravity. In physics, **work** is measured by lifting a **weight** a given **height**. In a frictionless world, a car traveling on flat terrain does "zero" work because there's no vertical displacement. Thanks to friction and our up and down bobbing (i.e. arms and head), we perform work when we walk. As a result, we burn fuel.

To increase the workload and heart rate intensity, and to burn more calories, it's advantageous to walk up an incline against gravity. Unfortunately, if you live in Delaware (highest elevation = 442 feet), you're not going to have much incline to work against. The same holds for those of us living in Kansas, Nebraska, Chicago and New Orleans where outdoor walking is a flatland experience. The steep streets of San Francisco, on the other hand, can overwhelm a deconditioned walker. However, on a treadmill, one touch of a button helps you create the right size *hills* for your heart to handle.

Then there's the weather to contend with–for example, training through the hot summers and the bitter arctic blasts of winter. Not to mention rain (100 inches a year in western Oregon). Have you ever estimated how many nice days a year you get for outdoor recreation?

Safety is another issue. Besides careless, malicious and intoxicated motorists, consider potholes, ruts in the road, dogs off the leash – and choking pollution. With all the smog, hydrocarbons, carbon monoxide and lead exhaust fumes in the air, you might wonder if you're better off exercising or sitting indoors on the couch.

> "About two years ago I had a heart attack and realized I needed to start exercising. So, I tried biking. It gave me a pain in the butt, and it was boring. I tried rowing; all I got were sore arms. Even regular walking didn't work for me, because when left to my own devices, I had to do the motivating. My subconscious took over, and if I was tired, I just sluffed off. The treadmill is different. It pulls me along. You've got to keep up or you're off the back rollers.
>
> So now I play games on the treadmill. I give myself little challenges – like seeing how many calories per minute I can burn, or how long I can hold a certain pace at a given elevation. Like tonight, I did four point seven miles per hour at ten percent grade. The interesting thing was that when I came home tired and wiped out, I asked myself, 'How am I going to get through a thirty minute workout?' But ten minutes from the end of that workout I felt like extending it. I wound up doing forty minutes. Now I feel great."

> **John Graner**
> Studio City, CA
> Regional Director,
> Prudential-Bache Securities
> **Jan '87:** Heart Attack
> **Feb '87:** 2 mph, 0% grade
> **Apr '89:** 4.7 mph, 10% grade

Maybe the most popular factors favoring treadmill exercise are **time** and **convenience**. How much time can you give to exercise? How much time do you waste getting ready to exercise? Lastly, how convenient is it to exercise?

Most of us find it difficult to set aside an hour every day for our constitutional walk. Yet watching 30 minutes of Jane Pauley (**NBC Today**) while treadmilling before your morning shower is not lost time. By the way, 30 treadmill-minutes with Jane can benefit you more than 60 minutes of stop-and-go walking on the streets.

Still the question comes, "If you can watch Jane on a treadmill, why can't you watch her on a $300 rowing machine?" You can, but the picture keeps bobbing in and out of focus. Besides, the rowing machine does not provide weight-bearing exercise. Neither does a stationary bicycle or swimming. This is particularly critical for women and those of us concerned about osteoporosis (bone loss disease). In treadmill walking your bones are in vertical compression; this helps keep calcium in the bone, preventing porosity and subsequent fracture.

"I've sold thousands of exercise bikes and rowers and hundreds of treadmills. But when I follow up with my customers, they tell me the bikes and rowers are in the closet acting as coat hangers. The treadmills, they use daily."

> *Robert Jacobs*
> *Beverly Hills*

Most important, just about everyone can walk on a treadmill...including cardiac rehabilitation patients, non-athletic, sedentary people, hypertensive subjects, diabetics, blind people and people of all abilities and fitness levels. Treadmill exercise is the safest, most natural way to train consistently for improved health and longevity. This is why the world reknown **Pritikin Longevity Centers** use treadmill walking as their prime exercise modality for nearly all visiting clients. Some of Pritikin's exercise floors are equipped with line-ups of 85 or more Trotter Treadmills.

"At Pritikin, the exercise we rely most on is treadmill walking because it utilizes the largest muscles – the hips and thighs – to accomplish the most total workload."

> *Dr. Tom Anderson*
> *Director Medical & Exercise*
> *Pritikin Longevity Center*
> *Santa Monica, CA*

The bottom line on treadmill training is "quality of life". Sure a treadmill will help strengthen your bones and tune up your heart. It will also raise your metabolism and trim your fat. If your blood pressure and stress levels are high, a treadmill will help you keep things under control. Simply put, treadmills add a new energy and zest to life. It may just be the perfect natural high.

TEN REASONS TO TRAIN ON A TREADMILL

The most natural physical exercise for the human body is walking. The most natural piece of home exercise equipment is a treadmill designed for walking.

1. **Convenience:** Anytime, day or night. Weekdays or weekends. Forget babysitters and your guilt in leaving the family behind. Just excuse yourself from the livingroom for 30 minutes!

2. **Time Utilization:** Catch the news. Workout while dinner is cooking or during a telephone conversation. Thirty minutes of TV treadmilling a day can burn 30 extra pounds of fat in a year.

3. **Natural Creativity:** On a treadmill, you simply put one foot in front of the other. This completely frees your mind to explore new thoughts.

The Pros and Cons of Home Exercise Equipment

HOME EXERCISE EQUIPMENT	ADVANTAGES	DISADVANTAGES
Rowing Machines **Summary:** Puts excessive stress on knee joints, plus they have one of the highest drop-out rates of home exercise equipment.	• Relatively inexpensive • Good cardiovascular workout	• Users susceptable to sore knees due to rubbing of tendons and ligaments near the knee cap • Very strenuous on the upper body
Stationary Bicycles **Summary:** Favor experienced bicyclists. Many novices suffer from saddle soreness and boredom.	• Relatively inexpensive • Good cardiovascular workout • Tones leg muscles • Good for TV watching	• Does little for upper body • Not weight bearing • Uncomfortable to sit on for extended periods • Can produce leg soreness for beginners
Cross-Country Ski Machines **Summary:** Many consumers who initially think they will "grow into" using this apparatus do not.	• Relatively inexpensive • Good cardiovascular workout • Tones the entire body • Weight bearing	• The average person is not comfortable on these devices. They require a fair degree of athletic coordination which most amateur, armchair athletes do not possess.

HOME EXERCISE EQUIPMENT	ADVANTAGES	DISADVANTAGES
Stair Climbers **Summary:** Can overstress the thighs, calves and Achilles tendons causing early fatigue and soreness. Potential tripping hazard. Over all, too much concentration, not enough enjoyment.	• Weight bearing • Good cardiovascular workout	• Fairly expensive • Potential tripping hazard • Quick fatigue of thighs and lower legs plus soreness of calves and Achilles tendon • Too strenuous for many
Weight-Lifting Apparatus **Summary:** Strengthens and tones muscles.	• Excellent muscle toner • Helps maintain high metabolism • Excellent compliment to aerobics • Equipment is long-lasting • Training time is not excessive	• Does not qualify as aerobic exercise • Not recommended for hypertensive individuals • By itself, not a great calorie burner
Non-Motorized Treadmills **Summary:** Do not provide the user a comfortable, natural walking gait.	• Relatively inexpensive • Weight bearing	• Feels uncomfortable • Difficult to walk on • Sore feet probable • Herky-jerky motion • Poor mechanical reliability • Not very enjoyable
Motorized Treadmills **Summary:** There is no better equipment for fitness training than a high-quality treadmill.	• Weight bearing • Easy learning curve • Excellent cardiovascular workout • Great for weight loss • Wide range of capabilities • Relaxing • Minimum time commitment	• More expensive • Depending on manufacturers' design and construction, mechanical reliability can be poor or excellent (see Ch. 4)

"In the old days, if I needed an excuse not to exercise, I always had the weather: 'It's too hot, too humid, too rainy or too cold.' With a treadmill, there's no excuse. Every night it's consistently there."

> *Wayne McCarty*
> *Manager, Carolina Fitness*
> *Charlotte, N.C.*

4.   Cold, Wind and Rain: All treadmill workouts are at the right temperature and humidity. From your picture window, watch the storms blowing.

5.   Feet, Ankles and Knees: The engineered slant of most roads (for rain runoff) can aggravate the ankles, knees and hips. Often this results in tendonitis and muscle inflammations. On a treadmill each foot lands true and square.

"Knee surgery left me without any cartilage tissue on my right side. I feel it when I run, especially on uneven road surfaces. That's why I train in my basement at night on a treadmill. It's the best way I know to get a consistent daily workout."

> *Brian Lyman*
> *Former Football Player*
> *Treadmill Walker*

6.   Capability: Looking for a good hill or nearby mountain to train on? Set the incline of your treadmill at 10% to 15% and hit the slopes.

7.   Entertainment: Invite friends and relatives to a non-fattening treadmill party at your home. The difference between crunching Doritos by the TV and crunching calories on the treadmill can easily be 200 calories per person.

8.   Sleep: The quality of your sleep is proportional to the number of calories you burn in a day (up to a certain limit). That's why a half hour of treadmilling during the day may help you cut back on sleep at night.

9.   Traffic and Pollution: Why face discourteous motorists and monoxide exhausts? Instead, smell the aroma of dinner during your evening treadmill workout.

10.   Stray Dogs: Hopefully, there won't be canine teeth snapping at your legs while treadmilling in your bedroom.

"I like to watch the first reaction of customers when they get on a tread-mill. Most of them smile. They love it. It's a different face than you see on a rower or bike."

> *Marc Dubois*
> *Store Owner, Fitnessland*
> *Toronto, Canada*

Chapter 2

BASIC TRAINING

Fundamental Treadmill Technique: footwork, posture, warm-ups and cool-downs, and supplemental muscle-toning exercises

From an energy standpoint, walking out–of–doors and walking on a treadmill burn about the same number of calories – assuming the same speed and slope. Biomechanically, there isn't all that much difference either – with one exception. On a treadmill, the walker's leading leg is consistently being transported backwards under the body; hence it is critical to develop a sense of timing and a regular natural stride in order to maintain proper balance and rhythm.

"The treadmill walks me. It's not like I'm the sole motivator. With a treadmill, I have a walking partner."

| *John Graner*

For someone not acquainted with walking on a moving treadmill belt, the initial feeling may be one of awkwardness. Novice treadmillers usually tighten up as they lean over their shoes, searching for a new center of gravity. Sweaty palms start groping for the handrails and the feet land flat-footed, *ka-plunk* style.

To think, we all learned heel-toe walking way back before kindergarten. The problem is that as a beginner on a treadmill, you may set the ball of your foot down way too soon directly under your body (instead of extending the leg with a good heel plant). Immediately, the belt pulls your foot back underneath your body, causing you to lurch forward off balance. This sets you up for your next misstep, and every step thereafter has you leaning forward in a falling position.

Yet a treadmill novice can turn into an expert quickly. The key is learning to relax. Remember, you know how to walk! You've been doing it since age one. If you find yourself semi-spastic on a moving treadmill belt, picture yourself walking naturally down the street. Extend each leg a few feet out in front of you and take longer strides. Let the belt pull your foot back to you – instead of you trying to force it back on your own power. Soon you'll be walking comfortably with a natural gait. Have faith!

WALKING POSTURE

About 85% of all Americans experience some type of back problem in life. Many of these problems stem from poor walking posture. However, by practicing the pointers which follow, all of us can improve our walking gaits – both on and off the treadmill.

POINT 1   *Focus straight ahead. You should be able to balance a book on your head while walking.*

POINT 2   *Walk with both your shoulders on a level plane so as not to tilt either right or left.*

POINT 3   *Walk tall with an erect posture; support your weight directly over your feet. No slouching!*

POINT 4   *Swing your arms to and fro in the direction of travel. Keep your elbows in close to your sides.*

POINT 5   *Your feet should point straight ahead enabling you to walk straight down an imaginary six-inch wide balance beam.*

POINT 6   *Land on your heel, with your leg extended in its natural forward position. As you begin to transfer your weight forward, roll over the ball of your foot and push off your toes. This is called heel-toe walking.*

TUNING UP YOUR TREADMILL TECHNIQUE

Many novice treadmillers look half-petrified stepping onto a moving belt. Even experienced walkers sometimes appear awkward. To improve your mechanics, consider these suggestions.

Mounting A Treadmill. If you look down at the "side shoulders" of a well-designed treadmill, you'll notice a wide strip with a non-slip surface. This shoulder is your "foot pad" and "landing strip" for starting and ending your workouts. By stepping from the "shoulder" onto the belt after the machine starts up, your knees and joints will not receive a herky-jerky start-up jolt. Plus, it puts less wear-and-tear on the motor and bearings. Likewise, when dismounting the treadmill, place one foot at a time on the "foot pads." As a safety precaution, always hold on to the handrails when mounting and dismounting your treadmill.

Body Position. Good treadmill walkers extend their legs forward enough, keeping their weight over their feet. This prevents their feet from landing too soon and stubbing into the moving belt, causing the body to lurch forward.

Head Position. Pick out an object at eye level on the wall ahead of you; stare at a poster; look at a picture; examine your nose, eyes and smile in a mirror in front of you. Playing these little games will relax you and help keep your head in a level position.

Heel Strike. Concentrate on landing on the back edges of your heel. The heels of most walkers strike at about a 10° greater angle with the horizontal plane than those of runners. Either way, running or walking, you should be able to slide a thin wedge in under your shoe at the moment your heel impacts the moving belt.

Your Best Positioning: Forward or Aft. Ever notice the positions people take on a treadmill belt? Some love to push right up against the front display panel. Others like to live dangerously on the back-end rollers. Are you a "Display Kisser" or a "Back-Door Roller"? The ideal location to "hang out" is two-thirds of the way forward on the belt – well ahead of the rear rollers. This gives you plenty of free space up front, plus a little cushion to fall back on in case you lose "ground" on a moment's hesitation.

Letting Go. When you feel insecure on a treadmill, your instinct is to grab the side handrails. This is fine as a temporary measure. The problem comes when you lean on such a crutch consistently for support. First off, you're upsetting your natural rhythm because your arms are not in sync with your legs. Secondly, you're decreasing the workload and burning less calories. In effect, you're cheating at a reduced workload. To break away from using the side rails as crutches, reduce the treadmill speed until you are comfortable with your walking technique and both arms are swinging freely.

Working With a Partner. One way to tune up your treadmill posture is to work one-on-one with a partner. Critique each other as you take short turns walking on the treadmill. Things to look for...head position (side view), heel-toe action (side view), arm swing (side and front views), body position (side view), shoulder levelness (rear view), straight-line foot placement (front view) and erect posture (side view). This simple exercise may teach you more about your walking posture than you've known all your life.

STRENGTHENING AND STRETCHING THE SUPPORTING MUSCLES

To maintain an injury-free treadmill training program, your musculoskeletal system must stay tuned up. Otherwise you're going to be vulnerable to orthopedic problems. Summarized below are exercises to tone your most important muscle groups.

Abdominal Muscles. The abdominal muscles play a critical role in maintaining good overall posture. Weak abdominals let the pelvis tilt forward and the lower back to arch which can cause accompanying lower-back and spinal problems. The easy and effective way to strengthen your upper and lower abdominals is to lie flat on your back, knees bent with your heels 12 inches from your posterior and your arms crossed over your chest. Now slowly curl forward until your elbows touch your thighs. Keep your neck relaxed and chin tilted slightly down toward your chest. How many you can do in a minute isn't nearly as important as how many you do in a day. Slow repetitions (two seconds up, two seconds down) let you work against gravity longer. This overloads the muscles more effectively and strengthens them faster. Fast sit-ups do not necessarily produce stronger muscles. Quality sit-ups build strong abdominals.

Thighs. The thighs (quadriceps) are the largest muscles in the human body, and they are the ones most crucial in walking. To tone and strengthen your thighs, you can workout on weight training machines, ride a bike, train on a stepping devise - or best of all, walk on an inclined treadmill.

Calves and Hamstrings. Walking uphill tends to tighten the calves and hamstring muscles. Muscle flexibility can be restored by stretching daily. Two ideal times to stretch are after your initial walking warm-up and after your final cool-down when your muscles are warm and pliable. *Static* stretches work best as opposed to *ballistic* or bouncing stretches which can tear soft connective tissue. In static stretches, you move into a stretching position until slight tightness begins to occur; then hold the stretch and concentrate on relaxing the muscle for about 20 seconds. Pain should not be felt!

Upper Body Strength. If you're wondering what upper body strength has to do with treadmill walking, realize that about 25% of your walking power comes from the thrust of the arms, chest and shoulders. To add more *horsepower* to your *walking engine,* you can lift weights or simply do push-ups and pull-ups. **Caution:** Individuals diagnosed as hypertensive or borderline hypertensive should be cautious in their weight-training or strength development programs. Do not hold your breath when lifting weights and do not grip objects in a static contraction (isometrics) for too long. Both of those acts can increase your blood pressure considerably.

Buttocks. To firm up your gluteus maximus (posterior), spend time walking "steep hills" on your treadmill. These muscles help to straighten the hip joint and are used extensively in walking uphill and in taking long strides.

FOOTCARE SUGGESTIONS

No matter where you walk, inside or outside, as your body temperature increases, feet begin to perspire; friction increases; hot spots start to occur – and before long, you're on your way to walking on a bubbly blister. To keep your feet happy: (1) Break in new shoes gradually. Wear them for short, low-intensity workouts for at least a week. (2) Wash your feet often and dry them thoroughly after showers, especially between the toes. (3) Before slipping on socks for a workout, coat your feet with cornstarch (expensive foot powders are not necessary). The "Shake & Bake" method works great (feet get inserted into a plastic bag of cornstarch). (4) Wear comfortable, moisture-absorbing socks. Socks of pure wool and cotton do not always hold their shape. Cheap tube socks don't either. Socks combining synthetic (stretch) and natural fibers (water-absorbing) generally work best. (5) Try foot massages – either with a partner or solo. (6) Inspect your feet after long, hard treadmill workouts; then wash, dry and powder them (cornstarch) thoroughly before putting on clean socks.

Many people think of stretching as the ideal way to warm-up before an aerobic exercise. Unfortunately the human body does not agree. The purpose of a warm-up is to let the body adjust gradually – without shock – to an increased workload. This is best accomplished when the large muscle groups adjust to low intensity work, causing a gradual increase in breathing and heart rate and a corresponding rise in core temperature (muscles become more pliable). At the same time, major blood vessels dilate, allowing for increased circulation. Such adaptations happen in five minutes of slow, moderate walking.

Similarly, a de-activation cool-down is important after an intense aerobic workout to stabilize blood pressure, flush carbon dioxide and lactic acid out of the muscles, and to help lower the body's temperature. This can prevent muscular stiffness and light-headedness later on. A good cool-down can be slow walking for five or more minutes. Then stretch! That's when your tight muscles need it most – after your aerobic cool-down. Specific treadmill walking warm-ups and cool-downs will be addressed in Chapter 5.

STRETCHING

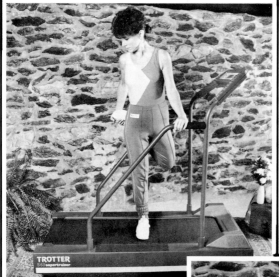

■ ■ ■

THIGHS: Clasp the instep of your right ankle with your left hand and hold for 20 seconds. Reverse arm and leg positions and repeat. NO PAIN! To stretch the inner thighs, assume the leaning position shown and hold without pain for 15-20 seconds.

NOTE: When stretching on a treadmill, one should always disconnect the power plug to prevent an accidental start-up.

CALVES & THIGHS: *The calves are stretched by pointing the toes up on a 45 degree angle while balancing the feet in a fulcrum position on the side frame of your treadmill. The hamstrings are stretched when leaning forward to touch the foot. Reach without pain!*

NOTE: When stretching on a treadmill, one should always disconnect the power plug to prevent an accidental start-up.

POSTURE

PROPER TREADMILL POSTURE: *(1) head is straight, (2) shoulders are level, (3) body is tall, (4) arms swinging freely, (5) feet point forward (single-track style) and (6) heel-toe, rock-n-roll motion!*

SINGLE VS. DOUBLE-TRACK WALKING: *By walking a "straight line path," you can increase your stride length by 5% to 10% with hardly any extra effort.*

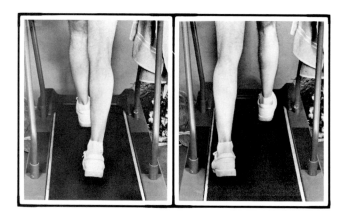

▪ ▪ ▪
STRADDLE START: *By using the "side shoulders" as your "stepping pad," your start-ups will be a lot smoother and safer.*

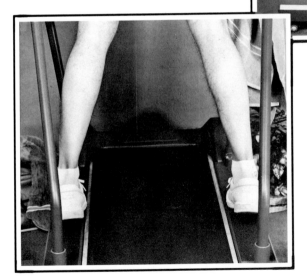

POSITION

■ ■ ■

THE TWO-THIRDS RULE:
Where do you make your home on the treadmill; front, middle or rear? The ideal position is two-thirds forward, well ahead of the rear rollers as Dr. Robert Neeves demonstrates in the photograph below.

HOLDING THE HANDRAILS: *People who hold handrails burn significantly less calories. Reason? Their upper bodies are stationary and the work necessary to fight gravity is less.*

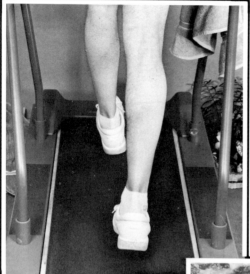

HEEL STRIKE: The foot lands on the outside corner of the heel. Check your heel strike by examining your shoes. If they're worn out on the outer back edges, you're landing well!

FOOT FOLLOW THROUGH: The legs should extend well ahead of the body; the front of the treadmill should permit full follow through.

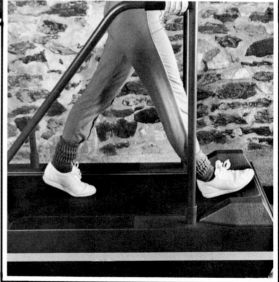

Chapter 3

THE PRINCIPLES OF TREADMILL TRAINING

What every treadmill enthusiast should know before starting a treadmill training program.

All exercise programs are defined by four primary parameters: (1) **type** of exercise, (2) **duration** of workout, (3) **intensity** of workout, and (4) **frequency** of training. Often these variables are abbreviated **TDIF**. For treadmill exercise, **TDIF** translates as follows:

Type: Three basic **types** of treadmill exercise exist: running, jogging and walking.

Duration: The **length** of any treadmill workout can range from several minutes to over an hour. Typically, an average treadmill workout, including a warm-up and cool-down, lasts 30 to 45 minutes.

Intensity: The rate of doing work on a treadmill is defined by the exercise intensity. The operating speed and elevation of a treadmill determine the intensity for any given person. The higher the intensity, the higher the resulting heart rate. Most treadmill workouts can be classified as **high**, **medium** or **low** intensity.

Frequency: The ideal number of workouts per week varies depending on one's goals; **three** for cardiovascular conditioning – **six** for weight loss – and **four** to **five** for general health.

Question: Of the four parameters – TDIF – which is most important?

Answer: One physiologist might argue that **intensity** is most important because hitting your target heart rate is critical for achieving an aerobic training effect and for increasing cardiovascular endurance. On the other hand, an epidemiologist could make a case in favor of **duration** and **frequency** based on studies that support the fact that people who exercise on a consistent basis – regardless of their heart rate intensity – live longer, healthier lives. On this same basis, one could say that the **type** of exercise is most critical, because if the individual selects the wrong type of exercise, his or her chance of maintaining that exercise program is essentially nil.

TWO CHOICES: TREADMILL RUNNING
AND TREADMILL WALKING

Two things that can make an exercise **wrong** for you: (1) injury potential and (2) psychological burnout. Consider, for example, choosing between the two basic **types** of treadmill exercise, **running** and **walking**. The "pros" and "cons" are many, but the real facts are hard to argue. Treadmill walking is a lot more comfortable than running on a treadmill – at least for the vast majority of people. To understand why, examine the accompanying chart.

TREADMILL WALKING	TREADMILL RUNNING
Positives • Easy on the joints • Impact landing is 1/2 to 1/3 that of running • Easy on hips, back, and spine • Psychologically non-threatening • Target heart rate easily achieved walking uphill • Can burn 500 to 1000 calories per hour • safe for obese people • Requires minimal pre-conditioning • Excellent leg muscle toning • Employs upper body muscles • Minimal stiffness and muscle flexibility loss • Perfect for long-slow-distance fat burning • Creates a natural high • Weight bearing exercise • Easy to do at any age • Low burnout rate • Easier to adjust the workload and intensity • Adaptible at any level of ability **Negatives** • Conditioning takes longer at low-intensity levels • Psychological adjustment for those in the "fast lane"	**Positives** • Excellent cardiovascular conditioner • Burns calories fast • Weight bearing exercise • Creates a natural high • Excellent leg muscle toning • Time-efficient (quick workouts) **Negatives** • More stressful on knees, back, ankles and hips than walking • Higher injury rate • Higher drop out rate • Not appropriate in certain heart disease/ orthopedic cases • Can reduce hamstring flexibility • Psychologically threatening to many people • Not appropriate for obese people • Does not feel natural to many people

CASE HISTORY

Dr. Sara Jane Bates is principal of Oaklea Middle School (Junction City, Oregon). Around age 30, she joined the jogging craze and built up to 40-mile training weeks before running her first marathon. By age 42, she had had enough running-induced joint inflammations to respect her doctor's orders, "Stop pounding the pavement!" Now she treadmills 12 to 15 miles per week in her finished basement, walking at 12% grade, 3.7 to 4.0 mph, at a target heart rate of 130 to 150 beats per minute. She doesn't miss running outside one bit (it rains over 100 days a year in western Oregon). Sara Jane has only one problem; she has to share her treadmill with husband Barry. After all, he bought the machine for the house in the first place.

WHY TREADMILL WALKING
SATISFIES THE "TDIF" ACID TEST

In every respect, *treadmill walking* offers a simple and safe way of earning great grades on your personal **TDIF** *report card.* Here's why!

Type: Treadmills are designed for natural movements in the weight-bearing position resulting in large caloric expenditures. You couldn't ask for a safer way to control body fat, blood pressure, stress and blood serum cholesterol.

Duration: In the home environment, treadmills enable relatively long uninterrupted workouts (30 to 60 minutes) while you're watching TV, talking on the phone or simply keeping an eye on things from a central location. **Note:** Treadmill walking workouts lasting even five or 10 minutes still have value because as an activity they contribute to your total daily expenditure of calories.

Intensity: Many walkers complain about not being able to reach elevated heart rates while walking. This is true on flat terrain; but on an inclined treadmill, you can hit your target heart rate quite easily.

Frequency: Treadmills take the sting out of winter and the heat out of summer. Weather is no longer an excuse to skip a day. With a treadmill, you can train consistently every day of the year.

THE CONCEPT OF
ADJUSTED WORKLOAD

Wouldn't it be convenient to have a single number which measures both **treadmill speed** and **treadmill elevation**? This way you could compare different workouts at a variety of speeds and elevations.

By using a new term called **Adjusted Workload**, you can now estimate the combined effect of **speed** and **elevation** instantaneously at any point during a workout. All you need to do is add your treadmill walking speed to one-tenth the value of your treadmill elevation as shown in the equation below:

$$AW = S + E/10$$

where "**S**" is the speed in miles per hour and "**E**" is the percent elevation expressed as a percentage integer. For instance, if you were walking at 4.2 mph on a 3% grade, then your Adjusted Workload (**AW**) could be approximated as follows:

$$AW = 4.2 + 3/10 = 4.2 + 0.3 = 4.5 \text{ mph}$$

In terms of energy expenditure, this is about the same as slowing down on a steeper hill – for instance, walking 3.7 mph at 8% elevation (**AW** = 3.7 + 0.8 = 4.5 mph). So in effect, **a 1% elevation increase creates about the same workload increase as a 0.1 mph speed increase.**

The **AW** equation **does not** apply to treadmill running; **nor** does it apply to treadmill walkers who consistently hold onto the handrails, thereby negating the effect of gravity. Furthermore, the **AW** equation is not a good fit for treadmill walkers who are unaccustomed to walking at moderately steep inclines (7% to 15% grade). If you are in this category, you will find a 1% increase in elevation considerably more stressful than a 0.1 mph speed increase. However the more you train at steeper grades, the closer your body will respond to the **AW** equation, $AW = S + E/10$. Until that time, you can use a modified form of the equation to estimate your Adjusted Workload: $AW = S + E/5$. In this formula, elevation gets weighted more heavily; in other words, it takes a 0.2 mph speed change to offset a change of only 1% in elevation.

The Adjusted Workload (**AW**) is also useful in estimating treadmill heart rates. For normal, healthy people training in the target zone (60% to 85% MHR), **a one-tenth of a mile per hour increase in adjusted workload causes a heart rate increase of three to five beats per minute** – depending on that particular person's cardiorespiratory condition. Fitter people tend to increase only **three** BPMs for every 0.1 mph increase in adjusted workload. A less fit person could expect to see a **five** BPM increase for every 0.1 mph increase in AW.

Example: John is completing his treadmill warm-up at 3 mph @ 3% grade at a heart rate of 100 BPM. How should he increase the speed and elevation to hit his target training rate of 128 BPM?

Answer: John is looking for a 28 BPM increase in his heart rate (from 100 to 128 BPM). Assuming he's of average aerobic fitness, he will probably experience about a **four** BPM increase for every 0.1 mph or 1% grade increase. Hence, any combined increase in speed and elevation which raises John's AW by 0.7 mph (7 x 4 = 28) will probably put John close to 128 BPM during excercise.

3.0 mph @ 3% grade = 3.3 mph (AW) @ 100 BPM   WARM-UP
4.0 mph @ 0% grade = 4.0 mph (AW) @ 128 BPM   JOHN'S
3.7 mph @ 3% grade = 4.0 mph (AW) @ 128 BPM   TRAINING
3.2 mph @ 8% grade = 4.0 mph (AW) @ 128 BPM   OPTIONS

FINE TUNING "TDIF" FOR SPECIFIC TRAINING GOALS

How can you adjust **TDIF** to accomplish specific training goals? Let's take a look at three examples.

For Weight Loss. The key is burning fat slowly over a long duration. In a treadmill workout, this means walking **longer** at a **lower intensity**. In other words, **walk for time, not for speed**. In 45 minutes of moderate-paced walking, a 150-pound person can burn 350 Calories – mostly stored fat. In 20 minutes of high-speed walking, that same person might burn 200 Calories – partially stored fat, partially muscle glycogen and blood sugars. Which is better: 200 Calories at high speed, or 350 Calories slow and easy?

Furthermore, to lose weight, the exercise **frequency** needs to be greater. It's difficult to lose weight walking three days a week. **Recommendation:** For weight loss, slow down on the treadmill and extend your workouts to a longer duration – and try to get some walking in at least six days a week (review the P-2 **Weight Loss** program in Chapter 5).

> *"I used to be a crazy runner until I sprained my ankle. Then I put on some fast pounds and really fell out of shape. When I tried to run myself back into shape, it was the old story, 'I don't want to run today.' Then I discovered the treadmill. In four months, I was burning five to six hundred Calories per (treadmill) session. I lost nineteen pounds. Now, I'm within two pounds of my college glory days. I've learned my lesson; now I can pass up the chocolate-chip cheesecake and double-cheese pizza."*

> **Karre Slafkin**
> **1984:** *Runner*
> **1985:** *Injured & Heavier*
> **1989:** *Happy Treadmill Walker*

For Cardiovascular Conditioning. To increase aerobic endurance, heart-rate intensity is the critical exercise factor. The workout needs to be continuous and of sufficient duration to maintain an **elevated heart rate in the target training zone**. You do not have to push yourself for a full 45 minutes. Thirty minutes is fine. Six days a week of hard, high-intensity treadmill walking can break you down. Three days a week is sufficient (review the P-3 **Cardiovascular Conditioning** program in Chapter 5).

For Long-Term General Health. Just burn the calories! You can do short-er, high-intensity treadmill workouts or longer, middle-intensity workouts. The former will tune your heart; the latter will burn your fat. Alternate these **short, high inten-sity** workouts with **long, middle-intensity** ones (day after day), and you'll develop a well-rounded, balanced training program geared for long-term health and body main-tenance.

TRAINING SUGGESTIONS

With all of the conflicting reports and innumerable myths floating around the fitness-exercise industry, it's no surprise that many people are confused about how to train on a treadmill. To help you train better, consider the following suggestions.

Go Hard, Then Easy. This is the best way to make progress; push yourself **hard** one day, and lay back **easy** the next. What is a **hard** treadmill workout? It's any sustained effort which elevates your heart rate near its maximum tested capability – i.e. 70% to 85% of maximum achievable heart rate (MHR). What's **easy**? Anything that's relatively comfortable, that you can maintain for a long time – i.e. 50% to 65% of MHR. The key is learning to mix **shorter, faster** workouts with **longer, slower** ones on alternating days. Many call this **The Hard-Easy Principle of Training**.

24-Hour Recovery. The great walker of the 19th century, Edward Payson Weston, competed in six-day races at distances of 90 to 120 miles per day – day after day. Yet, he never pushed himself so hard one day that he couldn't come back the following day to repeat his performance. Think about that! If you're too sore to work out on consecutive days, you may have done yourself more harm than good.

No Pain, All Gain. You don't have to "kill" yourself to benefit in a treadmill walking program. If you're experiencing pain – stop! If you're looking for a painful experience – forget it! You can burn fat, tone muscles, tune up your heart and keep healthy and happy – all without pain.

Keep Climbing. You can certainly drive your heart rate up walking **fast** on a **flat** treadmill. You can accomplish the same by walking **slowly** (3.0 to 3.5 mph) on an inclined **slope**. Mechanically, the human body was designed as a 3.5 mph walking machine. If you don't believe it, try out a variety of speeds to see which feels the best. If you're like most walkers, you'll prefer 3.3 to 3.7 mph. This may not raise your heart rate above 100 BPM unless you add "elevation" to your workouts. With elevation, you can climb at a low speed and a high heart rate which helps both you and your treadmill live longer.

Water. During a 40-minute treadmill workout an average 150-pound walker can lose three pounds easily. That's not fat; it's water. If you're careless enough not to replace that fluid, you may become dizzy and light-headed. Together with the onset of dry skin, these may be your first danger signs of dehydration. To avoid problems, drink about a glass of fluid prior to, during and after your workout.

Multiple Daily Workouts. Is it better to train **twice** daily for shorter durations or **once** daily for an extended time interval? Actually both! The shorter, more frequent, multiple workouts help raise your 24-hour metabolism (weight loss); longer workouts increase endurance and burn fat. Ideally, try a variety of workouts. It's better for both your mind and your body.

DOWNHILL TREADMILL WALKING

Some treadmill manufacturers are now boasting about a new feature – negative incline (treadmill slopes downhill to simulate real road conditions). Anyone who has done any downhill training, walking or running, knows the feeling of constantly having to "put on the brakes" to fight gravity. The result: friction, hot feet, sore toes, and blisters, excessive knee jamming and sore thighs. Not much fun. Plus, the total workload is reduced while going downhill, creating less of a cardiovascular training effect. Hence downhill treadmill training suffers from both a biomechanical and cardiovascular standpoint.

"Downhill training increases the impact forces on the lower extremities to a dangerous level – and without providing any real training benefit."

Dr. Barry Bates
Director – Biomechanics Sports Medicine Lab
University of Oregon.

Supplemental Muscle Exercises. On a daily basis, do something for your major working muscles. They are your *workhorse*. Without well-toned thighs and calves, you'll struggle on steep inclines. Also, upper body tone helps your arm swing, which in turn improves work output and caloric burn. All it takes to tone muscles is about ten minutes a day – a few minutes for stretching and a few more for strengthening.

Consistency. For long-term health, consistency is the most critical factor in a treadmill walking program. That translates to **enjoyment**: physical, psychological… any way you look at it. Try to have some fun! Nobody ever maintained a lifelong training program they didn't enjoy.

Chapter 4

HARDWARE AND SOFTWARE

State-of-the-art equipment. Self-Programmed and Pre-Programmed Treadmills: The Trotter CXT and 540 Supertrainer. Purchasing a treadmill.

Centuries ago, the Greeks, Romans and Egyptians used forms of human powered treadmills to lift and transfer heavy objects. But credit for the invention of the "modern" treadmill officially goes to Sir William Cubitt in 1818. Sir William's treadmill was used to grind corn and grain manually – employing the inexpensive horsepower of convicted criminals.

FOR THE RECORD

The first records of bipedal locomotion date back 3.5 million years to imprints found in soft volcanic ash in Tanzanaya.

The first sneakers were made and worn by Amazon jungle Indians (1730's) who dipped their feet into bowls of tree sap before standing by a fire to heat and bond the rubbery sap onto their skin.

In 1910, Edward Payson Weston walked from Santa Monica, CA to New York in 88 days, averaging 41 miles a day – at age 71.

Now, 170 years later, tens of thousands of motorized treadmills operate each day in dens, bedrooms, home exercise rooms and health & fitness centers. We are in the midst of a fitness revolution in which the motorized treadmill has become the premier training tool in quality health clubs today.

STATE-OF-THE-ART MOTORIZED TREADMILLS

Take a solid sheet of 12 gauge (0.1 inch thick) steel, bend and weld it into a sturdy frame capable of housing a motor, an inertial flywheel, a pair of steel rollers (one front, one rear), a wooden platform and handrails. Then slip a durable belt over the rollers and platform; add one more motor to raise and lower the walking platform. Finally, tie the whole electronics system together with a microprocessor controlled from a digital display panel. Now, program into the microprocessor 75 fitness workouts including self-evaluation tests, weight loss programs and cardiovascular conditioning workouts. Put this all together and you have a Trotter 540 Supertrainer.

Subtract from the 540 Supertrainer its package of computer programs, and make a few adjustments in its digital display panel and frame assembly – and you have a slimmer, less expensive unit called the Trotter CXT (Cardiovascular eXercise Trainer). Either way – 540 Supertrainer or CXT – you're looking at state-of-the-art equipment.

THE SELF-PROGRAMMED TREADMILL: THE CXT MODEL

To understand the difference between a **self-programmed** and **pre-programmed** treadmill, let's take a workout on the CXT and 540 Supertrainer.

When you first walk up to the CXT, you'll notice its digital display control panel. This panel is your keyboard to training. For instance, to start up the CXT, step onto the treadmill's side pads (straddling the belt) and press the **START/STOP** button. Within seconds the treadmill belt will start up at 1.0 mph; this speed will appear in red electronic digits on the display panel.

If you press the **CYCLE** button, your elapsed **TIME** will show. For example, "1:02" indicates that you're one minute and two seconds into the workout. Press **CYCLE** again, and your cumulative walking (or running) distance displays. Hit **CYCLE** again, and your **PACE** reads out in minutes per mile (i.e. 4 mph **PACE** reads "15:00" minutes per mile). The display panel also shows the percent **ELEVATION**.

To vary the treadmill **ELEVATION** or **SPEED**, press the arrows above the words **ELEVATION** and **SPEED**. For example, to warm up, you should gradually increase the elevation and speed for about five minutes. Now, adjust the treadmill to your full exercise workload, and continue training at whatever aerobic capacity you feel is comfortably challenging.

Near the conclusion of your workout, slowly decrease the **SPEED** and **ELEVATION** to cool down. By touching the **START/STOP** button again, the CXT treadmill will come to a halt. Then ask yourself, "Was my CXT workout challenging? Could I handle a greater elevation or speed, or should I back off in intensity? How can I put more variety into my workouts? How would I modify my treadmill protocol to burn more fat? How will I measure my treadmill progress?"

After reading chapters 5, 6 and 7, you should be able to answer these questions. But first, let's take a few minutes to better understand the 540 Supertrainer treadmill and its pre-programmed training workouts.

THE PRE-PROGRAMMED TREADMILL: THE 540 SUPERTRAINER

As its name implies, this treadmill is a "super trainer." The 540 Supertrainer has the full capability of the CXT, plus it is programmed to be your *coach*. The 540 Supertrainer enables you to **self-evaluate** your state of fitness using a 20-minute, walking protocol (P-1 program). Based on your test results, you train at the appropriate fitness level based on **your** specific goals: **weight loss training** (P-2 program), **cardiovascular conditioning** (P-3 program), **speed training** (P-4 program) or long-term **health maintenance** (P-5 program).

All the Supertrainer programs are stored on a tiny microprocessor chip tied into the treadmill's electronic system. How you train is your choice – P2 for weight loss or P4 for speed. All you do is push a button and the treadmill automatically takes you through your choosen protocol. Besides the P-1, P-2, P-3, P-4 and P-5 programs, four other workouts are programmed into the 540 Supertrainer as described.

Any day you're not in the mood for a pre-programmed workout, simply turn on the 540 Supertrainer at your own pace and intensity. Even if you're in the middle of a computerized workout, you can override the computer during any segment of the workout simply by pressing the **SPEED** or **ELEVATION** buttons.

540 Supertrainer Programs**	Duration minutes	Total Caloric Burn(Workload)
P-1 Self-Evaluation	20	Low-Medium
P-2 Weight Loss	45	High
P-3 Cardiovascular	30	Medium
P-4 Speed Intervals	30	Medium
P-5 Maintenance	15	Low-Medium
P-6 5K Run	Varies	Medium
P-7 10K Run	Varies	High
P-8 The Pritikin Workout	45	High
P-9 Hill-Interval Training	45	High

**The nine 540 Supertrainer programs are more fully described in Chapter 5.

TAKING YOUR FIRST COMPUTERIZED TREADMILL WORKOUT

Picture yourself straddling the belt of a 540 Supertrainer. Scanning the control panel, you'll notice a small rectangular **PROGRAM** button under the four-digit display. This button is your key to accessing any of the 75 computer programs in the 540 system.

If you press down on the **PROGRAM** button, **P1L1** will appear. That stands for **PROGRAM ONE (P1)** at **FITNESS LEVEL ONE (L1)**...**P1** being the 20-minute self-evaluation protocol and **L1** being the lowest of nine possible fitness levels (**L1, L2,...L9**).

If you then pressed **START** with the digital display showing **P1L1**, you'd automatically be taken through the complete 20-minute self-evaluation (**P1** Program) at the lowest fitness level possible (**L1**). If you're in reasonable shape, this **P1L1** protocol will be a snap for you. If you changed the "L" setting by pressing the **SPEED** button while the machine was displaying the **PROGRAM**, you would dial in higher intensity workouts such as **L2** on up to **L9**. If you selected **P1L9**, watch out! You're in for one fast and hard ride (5.5 mph at 12% grade).

During all computerized workouts, the **ELEVATION** and/or **SPEED** keep changing at pre-programmed time intervals. You start off with a low-intensity warm-up and finish easy with a cool-down. In between, you train at a workload based on your P-1 Self-Evaluation. This way, you always train at your proven fitness level. If at any time you feel you're in over your head, you can instantly decrease the workout intensity by lowering your **SPEED** or **ELEVATION** manually. The computer will respect your override until it's time for the next segment of the program. Then it steers you back into the program. If you need to override the computer several times in one workout, chances are you've misjudged your fitness level.

SELECTING A TREADMILL; SELECTING A DEALER
What you should know before buying a treadmill!

Shopping for a treadmill isn't like going out to buy a car. You won't find a dozen dealerships and stacks of Consumer Reports. Often the consumer stands in an exercise equipment showroom in the midst of a jungle of chrome and steel, wondering which is the best equipment for his or her body; bikes, rowing machines, ski simulators, weight-training systems...should you spend $100? $300? $800? $2000? $4000? or $10,000?

The average consumer needs time with a floor salesperson who understands exercise physiology.

> "Consumers are confused because there's so much conflicting information out there. They come into my store asking, 'What do you say I have to do to get fit?' Everybody who walks into our showroom gets put onto a treadmill, regardless of what they came in to buy. We find that's the best way to educate the consumer about exercise physiology and their bodies."
>
> Marc Dubois,
> Owner, Fitnessland
> Toronto, Canada

Assume you're thinking about buying a treadmill, but you're not sure what to buy or where to get it. The advertisements for $800 treadmills at the local department store seem interesting, but you've never discovered one satisfied customer boasting about one of these cheaper units.

With some products you feel like you're paying for a brand name. With treadmills, you're paying for engineering design, quality components – and the warranty behind them with follow-up service. The point is that all motorized treadmills are not created equal. The reason why some treadmills are relatively cheap is that they are made that way. Unfortunately, they get worse with time.

Before buying a treadmill, you should gain some basic understanding about treadmill design features, operating procedures, performance capabilities, maintenance requirements, life expectancy, manufacturer warranties, safety considerations and dealer support services. This doesn't mean you need a degree in treadmill engineering. Just pay careful attention to the following points.

Essential Design Features. (a) Is the walking platform of adequate size? (b) Are the handrails practical? (c) Is the treadmill motor sized adequately? (d) Does the treadmill elevate electronically? (e) Does the belt run smoothly without hesitation and slip? (f) Are the mechanical rollers and bearings sized adequately and do they run quietly without chatter and excessive vibration? (g) Do the base and frame adequately support you? (h) Are the instrument readouts on the digital display accurate?

Operating Capabilities. The following treadmill functional capabilities are highly desirable: a wide range of operating speeds, ranging from 1 mph to 8 mph, and a motorized elevation adjustment which lets you work out at 10% grade or higher.

> ***Elevating Your Treadmill.*** Have you ever been in the middle of a treadmill workout, wishing to change the incline, but you didn't because it was too much of a hassle to get off the machine and interrupt your aerobic flow? This can be a real nuisance when you'd like to change elevation five or more times in a 30-minute treadmill session.
>
> Some economy treadmills use manual hand crank levers which can be rotated while you're working out. However, you still wind up spending too much of your workout time cranking a lever. But if your treadmill has a motorized, push-button incline, you'll use it more and benefit without the hassles.
>
> ***Example.*** When you consider that a 1% increase in treadmill elevation (grade) causes an average healthy person's heart rate to increase by three to five beats per minute, you'll soon realize how powerful a tool your auto-elevation control button really is. For instance, if you started warming up at 3% grade @ 100 BPM @ 3.5 mph, you could then drive your heart rate up into the target training zone by steadily increasing the elevation from 3% to 6% to 9% to 12% (and higher if necessary) without having to force an uncomfortable pace.

Maintenance and Life Expectancy. How long will your treadmill last? What parts will wear out first? What kind of maintenance is necessary to keep your machine running? If a treadmill manufacturer or dealer can't give you straight answers to these questions, start looking elsewhere!

Safety. How safe is your treadmill? Does it have side handrails to grab and hold onto (temporarily) in case you lose your balance during exercise? Does it have a footpad platform for mounting and dismounting? Does the front of your treadmill allow your feet to follow through completely without stubbing your toes on the motor guard?

Manufacturers Warranty. How will the treadmill manufacturer stand behind the product? Can you get a 1-year warranty on all parts and labor? Are parts readily available locally? Are there trained mechanics who can service your machine?

The Pitfalls of Many Motorized Treadmills	Desirable Treadmill Features
• Inconsistent belt speed resulting in a herky-jerky gait. • Inaccurate speed display (poor instrument sensors) yields inaccurate "distance" and "speed" readouts. • No auto-elevation control. • Front motor guard assembly impairs forward leg extension. • Treadmill noise (can cause hearing loss). • No side handrails for emergency stability. • Impractical handrails.	• Powerful motor • Non-skid foot pads • Side handrails • Heavy inertial flywheel • Computer training programs • Auto-elevation control • Low front-end profile for foot follow through • Accurate digital displays • Larger rollers for smooth operation

Selecting a Dealer

Today many retailers are trying to take advantage of the "treadmill & walking" explosion by marketing low-quality, budget treadmills in department stores and sporting goods shops. Many of these retailers do not understand treadmill technology, and for that reason, they offer little assistance to the consumer.

On the other hand, many fitness equipment specialty stores around America (and Canada) carry quality merchandise backed by quality sales and service staffs. These stores don't carry inexpensive treadmills because they're not interested in being full-time repair centers.

Basically you have a choice; you can buy a relatively inexpensive treadmill from a department store that's selling refrigerators and house paints, or you can go to someone who will help train you to insure your satisfaction.

Following are questions you might want to ask a treadmill salesperson to find out what they do and don't know about their product: **Why** do you believe in treadmill walking? **How** long have you been selling treadmills here? **Do** you train on a treadmill yourself? **If** something went wrong with my treadmill, say after four months, how would I get it fixed? **Do** you deliver, install and service this machine? **What** kind of extended warranty package do you or the manufacturer offer? **Can** you demonstrate exactly how this treadmill works? **How** would you recommend I get started on a treadmill walking program?

Before You Buy. (a) Find a salesperson who really knows treadmill technology by visiting the best fitness equipment specialty stores in your area. (b) Ask for an in-store treadmill demonstration to test drive the machine yourself. Compare the performance of one model to another at various speeds and inclines. (c) Inquire about customer service, delivery and installation, and extended service warranties. (d) Then, if you're satisfied, go ahead and "take the plunge." Chances are you'll be enjoying many years of happy, healthy treadmilling.

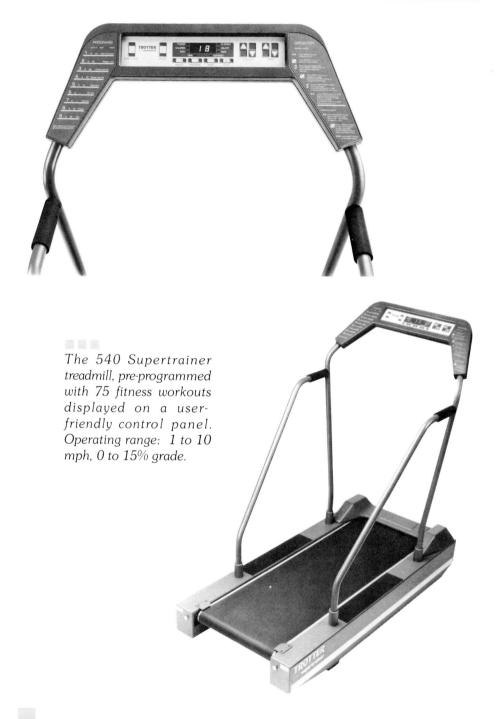

The 540 Supertrainer treadmill, pre-programmed with 75 fitness workouts displayed on a user-friendly control panel. Operating range: 1 to 10 mph, 0 to 15% grade.

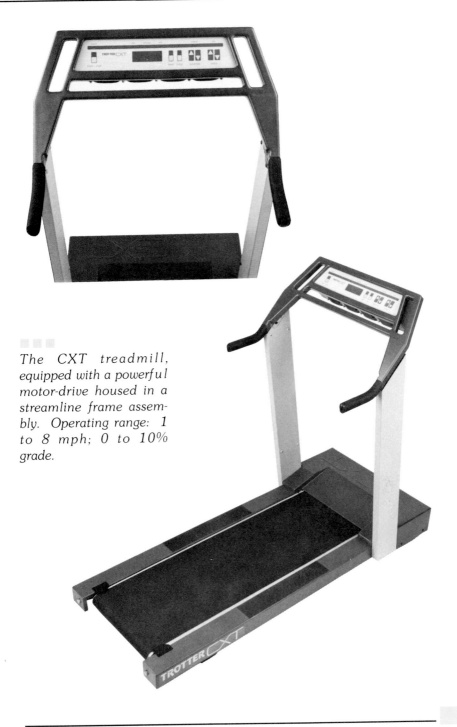

The CXT treadmill, equipped with a powerful motor-drive housed in a streamline frame assembly. Operating range: 1 to 8 mph; 0 to 10% grade.

LOOKING AHEAD

In the next two chapters of **Treadmill Walking** a variety of training workouts will be discussed in detail. Chapter 5 focuses on computerized training and Chapter 6 expands on a wide variety of creative treadmill workouts.

Whether you own a treadmill, train on a treadmill, or are seriously considering buying a treadmill, it is highly recommended that you read **both** Chapters 5 and 6 to learn more about treadmill training strategies.

THE MENU OF COMPUTER PROGRAMS: TRAINING ON AUTOMATIC PILOT

Self-Evaluation, Weight Loss, Cardiovascular Conditioning, Speed Training, Recovery Workouts, Pritikin Interval Training, 5K & 10K Runs and Walks.

A businessman stands in sweat clothes with hands on hips in front of his sparkling new treadmill wondering where to begin. Yesterday, a salesman had given him a quick demo...how to start the machine...how to walk on it...and how to make out the check. Now a day later, Mr. Consumer is scratching his head, thinking "hmmmm."

If this story sounds familiar, realize that many treadmill consumers don't understand what they've purchased. Although there are exceptions, most consumers really need more coaching on treadmill training.

This is why Trotter pioneered pre-programmed walking workouts inside the 540 Supertrainer treadmill. These workouts are controlled by the treadmill's computer which guides you in training. It gives you an easy, accurate way to self-evaluate your fitness level. Once you know your limits, you can select from a variety of workouts appropriate for your tested capacity. And all you need to do is push a button.

THE 540 SUPERTRAINER MENU OF PRE-PROGRAMMED WORKOUTS

P1	Self-Evaluation	(9 fitness levels)
P2	Weight Loss	(9 fitness levels)
P3	Cardiovascular	(9 fitness levels)
P4	Speed Interval	(9 fitness levels)
P5	Maintenance/Recovery	(9 fitness levels)
P6	5 Kilometer Workout	(6 fitness levels)
P7	10 Kilometer Workout	(6 fitness levels)
P8	Pritikin Intervals	(9 fitness levels)
P9	Hill Training	(9 fitness levels)

Overview. Before starting any treadmill walking program, it's a smart idea to establish your baseline fitness level. This can be accomplished using the 540 Supertrainer P-1 Self-Evaluation program. After doing the 20-minute P-1 walking test, you'll be able to classify yourself as a **white belt** (LEVEL 1), **black belt** (LEVEL 9) – or anything in between. From then on, simply train at your proven fitness level.

Objective. The P-1 Program is designed to help you predict your **Treadmill Walking Capacity** and **Fitness Level** for optimal future training.

How the Program Works. The 20-minute P-1 Self-Evaluation program starts with a six-minute warm-up, moves into a nine-minute testing period, and concludes with a five-minute cool-down. During the nine-minute testing period, the treadmill automatically increases both its SPEED and ELEVATION every three minutes. The real "acid test" is the 13th, 14th and 15th minutes when you're pushing at your maximum workload.

To pass this P-1 Self-Evaluation, you must complete the 15th minute: (1) without exceeding 85% of your maximum heart rate, and (2) without feeling discomfort, pain or abnormal symptoms of stress and fatigue. If you successfully complete the P-1 protocol at a given level (say level 6 or L6), then you're capable of training at that level (**L6** or **purple belt**). This logic applies at all levels, **L1** to **L9**.

Before taking the P-1 Self-Evaluation, you must first make a guess about your fitness level. To help you make your first "P1" guess, realize that a moderately fit person should be able to pass his/her **P1L4** protocol (green belt). If you guess reasonably well, you'd finish your 15th minute of the **P1** protocol at 75% to 85% of your maximum heart rate.

If you overestimate your level of fitness, your pulse might exceed the 85% limit – especially during the 4th or 5th interval of the workout. If this happens and you become breathless, don't try to be a hero by finishing the P-1 Self-Evaluation. Stop the test and wait a day or two before retesting yourself at a lower fitness level.

If you underestimate your fitness level, you'll finish the P-1 protocol with a low pulse (assuming you're not on medication). In this case, retest yourself in a day at the next highest fitness level. The following chart will give you a fair idea of the workloads involved at each fitness level.

A Word of Caution: *The 540 Supertrainer programs are not to be viewed as a substitute for a medically supervised treadmill tolerance test (stress EKG test). Taking the latter will help insure safe cardiac functioning under relatively high workload conditions. Should you feel any discomfort such as chest pains, chest pressure, shortness of breath or dizziness during any treadmill workout, stop immediately. These are warning signs that need to be discussed with your doctor. However, the likelihood of such an occurrence is very small for anyone successfully completing a comprehensive medical check-up and treadmill tolerance test.*

SELF-EVAL PROGRAM	FITNESS LEVELS	FITNESS COLOR	P-1 PEAK WORKLOADS
P1	L1	White	2.5 mph @ 4.0% grade
P1	L2	Yellow	3.0 mph @ 5.0% grade
P1	L3	Orange	3.3 mph @ 6.0% grade
P1	L4	Green	3.5 mph @ 7.0% grade
P1	L5	Blue	3.7 mph @ 8.0% grade
P1	L6	Purple	4.0 mph @ 9.0% grade
P1	L7	Red	4.5 mph @ 10.0% grade
P1	L8	Brown	5.0 mph @ 11.0% grade
P1	L9	Black	5.5 mph @ 12.0% grade

Which workload do you think you can handle? What's your fitness color...white, yellow, orange, green, blue, purple, red, brown or black?

Note: Do not conduct a P-1 Self-Evaluation if you have been diagnosed as having heart problems or suspect that you do. Consult with your doctor first, and if recommended, take a medically supervised treadmill tolerance test.

SUGGESTIONS FOR P-1 SELF TESTS

If you find yourself struggling on the P-1 self-test, immediately decrease the **SPEED** and **ELEVATION** to a comfortable level. You probably overestimated your fitness level. Also, avoid doing P-1 Self-Evaluations on consecutive days. The body needs recovery time when pushed to its limits. Lastly, do not attempt a P-1 Self-Evaluation directly after a meal!

HAVE YOU PASSED YOUR P-1 SELF-EVALUATION?

You can claim "success" on your P-1 Self-Evaluation if you can honestly answer "YES" to all three criteria below:

YES   NO   I completed P-1 without any pain.

YES   NO   During P-1, I could have conversed comfortably

YES   NO   Immediately following the fifth segment of the P-1 self-test, my exercise heart rate was **LESS THAN** 85% of its maximum capability!

To answer "yes" on the last condition, you need to take your heart rate precisely at the end of the fifth interval of the P-1 program. To pass your P-1 Self-Evaluation, your Exercise Heart Rate (at t=15 minutes) must be **LESS THAN** 85% of its **MAXIMUM RATE**.

Your Age-Predicted Maximum Heart Rate

Age	Max Heart Rate	To Pass P-1 Self-Test*
20	200 BPM	170 beats per minute
30	190 BPM	162 beats per minute
40	180 BPM	153 beats per minute
50	170 BPM	145 beats per minute
60	160 BPM	136 beats per minute
70	150 BPM	128 beats per minute

*Note: A simple formula for estimating your maximum heart rate (MHR) is MHR = 220-YOUR AGE. Realize however that this equation is merely an approximation. Your true maximum heart rate is best determined during a treadmill tolerance test. However, for purposes of determining **success** or **failure** on a P-1 Self-Evaluation test, it is permissible to use 85% of the age-predicted MHR simply for a **pass-or-fail** criterion.

SUMMARY: P-1 SELF-EVALUATION PROGRAM

Fitness Level	Belt Color		Elapsed Time (minutes)						
			0	3	6	9	12	15	20
L1	white	SPEED (mph) % GRADE	W A R M U P			2.0 2.0	2.2 3.0	2.5 4.0	C O O L D O W N
L2	yellow	SPEED % GRADE				2.4 2.5	2.6 3.8	3.0 5.0	
L3	orange	SPEED % GRADE				2.6 3.0	2.9 4.5	3.3 6.0	
L4	green	SPEED % GRADE				2.8 3.5	3.1 5.3	3.5 7.0	
L5	blue	SPEED % GRADE				3.0 4.0	3.3 6.0	3.7 8.0	
L6	purple	SPEED % GRADE				3.2 4.5	3.5 6.8	4.0 9.0	
L7	red	SPEED % GRADE	Note: All warm-ups and cool-downs are individually designed for each fitness level.			3.6 5.0	4.0 7.5	4.5 10.0	
L8	brown	SPEED % GRADE				4.0 5.4	4.4 8.3	5.0 11.0	
L9	black	SPEED % GRADE				4.4 6.0	4.8 9.0	5.5 12.0	

Speed (mph) and % grade shown for the third through fifth intervals of the self-test.

Overview. The two key factors in walking off fat are **time** and **consistency**. You don't have to walk super fast to burn fat. By backing off on the **intensity** and increasing the **duration** of your treadmill workouts, you will burn fat and preserve muscle. Maintained over a lifetime, this behavior will keep weight off permanently. This is the strategy behind the P-2 Weight Loss program: *medium* intensity, *long* duration. Some call this **long slow distance.**

Objective. The P-2 workout helps you burn fat at a relatively comfortable pace. For obese individuals, P-2 workouts are less stressful on the heart and joints than other higher-intensity workouts (i.e. P-3, P-4). Consistent P-2 training is a great way to prepare for future workouts at higher intensities.

How the Program Works. After a six-minute walking warm-up, the workload increases to a comfortable, steady-state level of 86% of your P-1 test performance. You work at this level for five minutes, after which the treadmill elevation increases causing your metabolism to peak. This peak period lasts two minutes, after which you return to your normal, steady-state walk for another five-minute interval. These brief two-minute "hills" help you burn more calories during your major five-minute intervals. A 45-minute P-2 workout consists of five such cycles (35 minutes) plus 10 minutes for warm-up and cool-down. In effect, it's like walking on five rolling hills to burn fat.

WEIGHT LOSS PROGRAM	FITNESS LEVELS	P-2 WORKLOAD RANGE
P2	L1	2.2 mph @ 3.0 — 4.0%
P2	L2	2.6 mph @ 3.8 — 5.0%
P2	L3	2.9 mph @ 4.5 — 6.0%
P2	L4	3.1 mph @ 5.3 — 7.0%
P2	L5	3.3 mph @ 6.0 — 8.0%
P2	L6	3.5 mph @ 6.8 — 9.0%
P2	L7	4.0 mph @ 7.5 – 10.0%
P2	L8	4.4 mph @ 8.3 – 11.0%
P2	L9	4.8 mph @ 9.0 – 12.0%

In a P-2 Weight Loss Workout, 77% of the time you are walking at 86% (or more) of your P-1 test performance capacity.

Suggestions For P-2 Training. If you are just starting a fitness walking program, the full 45-minute P-2 program can overstress you. Until you're comfortable training for 45 continuous minutes, cut back on your P-2 workout by dropping the last three exercise cycles; this saves you 21 minutes. This way, you'll benefit from 24 minutes of fat burn instead of 45 minutes of sore muscles.

How many P-2 workouts are necessary each week? Ideally, it would be great to complete **three** or **four**, preferably on alternate days, say **Mondays**, **Wednesdays** and **Fridays**. In between, do a P-3 or P-5 workout, or just walk outdoors and enjoy nature. The key is staying active daily.

WEIGHT LOSS & LIFESTYLE

The best way to lose weight (fat) and keep it off permanently is to increase your metabolism by becoming a more physically active person – for life! In doing P-2 workouts, you burn 300 (level 5) to 400 (level 7) Calories per workout (for a 160-pound person). Unfortunately one major midnight ice-cream raid on the "fridge" offsets that energy expenditure. However, by supplementing your treadmill training with some **simple lifestyle habits**, you can lower your body fat composition and keep unwanted fat from creeping back on. For starters, try working towards these lifestyle changes.

1. *Diets don't work. Increase your activity instead of just decreasing your fuel supply.*

2. *Eat more carbohydrates and less fat. "Carbos" are high-quality fuel. Fatty foods are fattening – not to mention their effect on arterial walls.*

3. *Eat early in the day – especially breakfast. Avoid late-night snacking!*

4. *Supplement your treadmill training with short walks every day: walks across the parking lot and walks to the store. Even a flight of stairs or a minute on the treadmill has value.*

5. *Think of food as fuel! Let hunger (not appetite) be your cue to refuel.*

6. ***Little changes** make the **big difference.** Quick weight loss is temporary weight loss. Go for **consistency** over the long haul.*

Fitness Level		Elapsed Time (minutes)				
		0 6	11	13	41	45
1	SPEED (mph) % GRADE	**W**	2.2 3.0	2.2 4.0		**C**
2	SPEED % GRADE	**A**	2.6 3.8	2.6 5.0	C C C C Y Y Y Y C C C C	**O**
3	SPEED % GRADE	**R**	2.9 4.5	2.9 6.0	L L L L E E E E	**O**
4	SPEED % GRADE	**M**	3.1 5.3	3.1 7.0	2 3 4 5	**L**
5	SPEED % GRADE	**U**	3.3 6.0	3.3 8.0		
6	SPEED % GRADE	**P**	3.5 6.8	3.5 9.0	In the P-2 program, the 7-minute cycle	**D**
7	SPEED % GRADE		4.0 7.5	4.0 10.0	repeats five times (35	**O**
8	SPEED % GRADE		4.4 8.3	4.4 11.0	minutes).	**W**
9	SPEED % GRADE		4.8 9.0	4.8 12.0		**N**

Program 3
CARDIOVASCULAR CONDITIONING

Overview. When aerobic activity is sustained at a fairly intense level, the heart muscle becomes stronger; the blood vessels respond better to increased circulation; and the overall oxygen transfer from the lungs to the circulatory system to the working muscles improves. Any aerobic exercise – walking included – produces this cardiovascular training effect. The key is working the heart at about two thirds (or more) of its maximum pumping rate. This can be achieved by walking very briskly with a high-energy arm swing (not particularly comfortable for most walkers) **or** by walking at a moderate pace up a mountain road or an incline. The P-3 program gives you the right-sized "mountain" for your heart to handle.

Objective. The P-3 program provides a high-intensity, 30-minute cardiovascular workout compatible with your P-1 self-evaluation performance.

THE CARDIOVASCULAR BENEFITS
OF P-3 WORKOUTS

By training consistently on the P-3 program, you will improve your chances of: (1) maintaining normal blood pressure; (2) improving collateral circulation throughout your heart muscle; (3) strengthening your heart muscle for maximum work output; (4) reducing your resting heart rate; (5) enhancing your HDL/LDL cholesterol ratio; (6) increasing muscle mass and decreasing percent body fat; (7) maintaining blood vessel elasticity; and (8) increasing your aerobic endurance and overall energy.

How the P-3 Program Works. The P-3 protocol begins with an easy four-minute warm-up, followed by a series of increasing **SPEED** and **ELEVATION** changes designed to put you at a target training rate. After reaching your peak workload, you begin slowing down gradually until the 26th minute. The remaining four minutes of the P-3 workout is your cool-down.

CARDIOVASCULAR PROGRAM	FITNESS LEVELS	AVERAGE WORKLOAD
P3	L1	2.4 mph @ 3.7% grade
P3	L2	2.9 mph @ 4.6% grade
P3	L3	3.1 mph @ 5.6% grade
P3	L4	3.4 mph @ 6.5% grade
P3	L5	3.6 mph @ 7.4% grade
P3	L6	3.9 mph @ 8.4% grade
P3	L7	4.3 mph @ 9.3% grade
P3	L8	4.8 mph @ 10.0% grade
P3	L9	5.3 mph @ 11.1% grade

During a P-3 Cardiovascular workout, you train at an intensity level averaging 93% of your maximum P-1 performance capability for 22 out of 30 minutes.

COMPARING P-2 AND P-3 WORKOUTS ON A 540 SUPERTRAINER

	P-2 WORKOUTS	P-3 WORKOUTS
Primary Benefit	Weight Control	Cardiovascular Conditioning
Exercise Intensity	Medium	High
Workout Duration	45 minutes	30 minutes
Rec'd Frequency	4 times/week	3 times/week
Calories Spent*	330	265
Advantages	Greater Caloric burn	Higher Intensity

*Based on **LEVEL 7** workout (P2L7, P3L7) for a 160-pound person.

SUMMARY: P-3 PROGRAM

Fitness Level		Elapsed Time (minutes)				
		0	4		26	30
1	SPEED (mph) % GRADE	**W**	2.2 3.0	2.5 4.0	2.2 3.0	**C**
2	SPEED % GRADE	**A**	2.6 3.8	3.0 5.0	2.6 3.8	**O**
3	SPEED % GRADE	**R**	2.9 4.5	3.3 6.0	2.9 4.5	**O**
4	SPEED % GRADE	**M**	3.1 5.3	3.5 7.0	3.1 5.3	**L**
5	SPEED % GRADE	**U**	3.3 6.0	3.7 8.0	3.3 6.0	
6	SPEED % GRADE	**P**	3.5 6.8	4.0 9.0	3.5 6.8	**D**
7	SPEED % GRADE		4.0 7.5	4.5 10.0	4.0 7.5	**O**
8	SPEED % GRADE		4.4 8.3	5.0 11.0	4.4 8.3	**W**
9	SPEED % GRADE		4.8 9.0	5.5 12.0	4.8 9.0	**N**

SPEED (INTERVAL) TRAINING

Overview. To increase your walking speed and aerobic capacity, it helps to periodically train at near-maximum effort in a series of hard-easy intervals in which you **push intensely** for short spurts – and then **relax** for recovery. Done weekly, such *interval training* will increase your: (1) tolerance for more strenuous workouts, (2) anaerobic capacity and (3) maximum walking pace.

Objective. The P-4 program pushes you to your maximum potential in a series of short intervals to help you adapt to higher workload capacities.

How the P-4 Program Works. Since *interval training* is fairly stressful on your cardiorespiratory system, a longer eight-minute warm-up is used in the P-4 program. Then it's time to fasten your seatbelt! Your first "Super Interval" is about to begin as the treadmill **SPEED** and **ELEVATION** quickly increase, requiring you to walk 10% faster than your P-1 peak speed. **Two** minutes later, the treadmill slows down (about 30%), giving you **three** minutes of "moving recovery" before your next speed interval. In a 30-minute P-4 workout you do four of these **HARD-EASY** intervals before your final cool-down stage.

INTERVAL PROGRAM	FITNESS LEVELS	MAX WORKLOAD (2 MINUTES)	RECOVERY WORKLOAD (3 Minutes)
P4	L1	2.8 mph @ 4.0%	2.0 mph @ 4.0%
P4	L2	3.4 mph @ 5.0%	2.4 mph @ 5.0%
P4	L3	3.6 mph @ 6.0%	2.6 mph @ 6.0%
P4	L4	3.9 mph @ 7.0%	2.8 mph @ 7.0%
P4	L5	4.2 mph @ 8.0%	3.0 mph @ 8.0%
P4	L6	4.5 mph @ 9.0%	3.2 mph @ 9.0%
P4	L7	5.0 mph @ 10.0%	3.6 mph @ 10.0%
P4	L8	5.6 mph @ 11.0%	4.0 mph @ 11.0%
P4	L9	6.2 mph @ 12.0%	4.4 mph @ 12.0%

The P-4 Speed Interval Program is a combination of **hard work** and **easy play**. The net result: your body learns to handle higher workloads.

Suggestions. (1) If you're starting a treadmill program, let your body adapt at lower-intensity training before trying P-4 interval workouts. Initially, train at lower speeds for longer duration (P-2 program). As your body conditions, try a P-4 workout at one fitness level below your P-1 tested capability – just to be safe. If you pass that, advance to a P-4 workout at your regular fitness level.

SUMMARY: P-4 PROGRAM

Fitness Level	Elapsed Time (minutes)								
		0	8	13	18	23	28	30	
L1	SPEED (mph) % GRADE	W A R M U P		2.8 - 2.0 - 2.8 - 2.0 - 2.8 - 2.0 - 2.8 - 2.0 4%--					C O O L D O W N
L2	SPEED % GRADE			3.4 - 2.4 - 3.4 - 2.4 - 3.4 - 2.4 - 3.4 - 2.4 5%--					
L3	SPEED % GRADE			3.6 - 2.6 - 3.6 - 2.6 - 3.6 - 2.6 - 3.6 - 2.6 6%--					
L4	SPEED % GRADE			3.9 - 2.8 - 3.9 - 2.8 - 3.9 - 2.8 - 3.9 - 2.8 7%--					
L5	SPEED % GRADE			4.2 - 3.0 - 4.2 - 3.0 - 4.2 - 3.0 - 4.2 - 3.0 8%--					
L6	SPEED % GRADE			4.5 - 3.2 - 4.5 - 3.2 - 4.5 - 3.2 - 4.5 - 3.2 9%--					
L7	SPEED % GRADE			5.0 - 3.6 - 5.0 - 3.6 - 5.0 - 3.6 - 5.0 - 3.6 10%--					
L8	SPEED % GRADE			5.6 - 4.0 - 5.6 - 4.0 - 5.6 - 4.0 - 5.6 - 4.0 11%--					
L9	SPEED % GRADE			6.2 - 4.4 - 6.2 - 4.4 - 6.2 - 4.4 - 6.2 - 4.4 12%--					

Overview. Some days you just don't feel up to a full workout. Whether it's due to overtraining the day before or cyclic chemistry, your body screams "Give me a break today!" So you sack out in the Lazy-Boy and watch the tube – until the Guilt Bug creeps up on the arm rest to remind you to workout. So what do you do? You either remain seated, or you hop on your 540 Supertrainer and "dial" P-5. The 15-minute P-5 workout will help you recover without overstressing your body. That night, you'll feel better for having moved yourself out of the Lazy Boy.

Six Good Times for a P-5 Walking Workout. (1) Tired from a difficult workout and don't feel like pushing too hard. (2) Feeling sluggish; just looking for a bare minimum workout. (3) Tuning up for a big event and don't want to overstress your body. (4) The day before your P-1 Self-Evaluation. (5) Coming back from an illness. (6) Short of time, but in need of a minimal workout.

Objective. The P-5 program is your minimal essential workout designed to let your body recover and maintain itself.

RECOVERY PROGRAM	FITNESS LEVEL	AVERAGE WORKLOADS
P5	L1	2.3 mph @ 3.0% grade
P5	L2	2.8 mph @ 4.1% grade
P5	L3	3.0 mph @ 5.0% grade
P5	L4	3.2 mph @ 5.8% grade
P5	L5	3.5 mph @ 6.6% grade
P5	L6	3.7 mph @ 7.4% grade
P5	L7	4.1 mph @ 8.3% grade
P5	L8	4.6 mph @ 8.9% grade
P5	L9	5.1 mph @ 9.9% grade

P-5 workouts are short and easy, yet they still put you in the target training zone.

SUMMARY: P-5 PROGRAM

Fitness Level			Elapsed Time (minutes)				
		0	3	9 MINS IN TARGET ZONE		13	15
1	SPEED (mph)	**W**		2.2	2.5	2.2	**C**
	% GRADE			3.0	4.0	3.0	
2	SPEED	**A**		2.6	3.0	2.6	**O**
	% GRADE			3.8	5.0	3.8	
3	SPEED	**R**		2.9	3.3	2.9	**O**
	% GRADE			4.5	6.0	4.5	
4	SPEED	**M**		3.1	3.5	3.1	**L**
	% GRADE			5.3	7.0	5.3	
5	SPEED			3.3	3.7	3.3	
	% GRADE	**U**		6.0	8.0	6.0	
6	SPEED	**P**		3.5	4.0	3.5	**D**
	% GRADE			6.8	9.0	6.8	**O**
7	SPEED			4.0	4.5	4.0	**W**
	% GRADE			7.5	10.0	7.5	
8	SPEED			4.4	5.0	4.4	**N**
	% GRADE			8.1	11.0	8.1	
9	SPEED			4.8	5.5	4.8	
	% GRADE			9.0	12.0	9.0	

Programs 6 and 7
FIVE AND TEN KILOMETER RUNS & WALKS

Overview. The P-6 and P-7 treadmill programs simulate "training on the road" by presenting you with a hilly **cross-country** race course. At various distances into your run or walk, the treadmill changes slope. Then, it's up to you to adjust your pace. A P-6 or P-7 workout is complete when you've completed five kilometers (3.1 miles) or ten kilometers (6.2 miles), respectively. How fast can you run or walk a treadmill 10K?

Objective. The P-6 and P-7 programs provide you with an excellent cardiovascular workout by challenging you to work against gravity on rolling 5K and 10K race courses.

PROGRAM 6 - THE 5K RUN OR WALK

DISTANCE (3.1 MILES)	LEVEL 1 GRADE	LEVEL 2 GRADE	LEVEL 3 GRADE	LEVEL 4 GRADE	LEVEL 5 GRADE	LEVEL 6 GRADE
.1	0.0%	0.0%	0.0%	0.0%	0.0%	0.0%
.1	1.0%	1.1%	1.2%	1.3%	1.5%	1.6%
.2	2.0%	2.2%	2.4%	2.7%	2.9%	3.2%
.3	0.0%	0.0%	0.0%	0.0%	0.0%	0.0%
.1	1.0%	1.1%	1.2%	1.3%	1.5%	1.6%
.1	2.0%	2.2%	2.4%	2.7%	2.9%	3.2%
.1	3.0%	3.3%	3.6%	4.0%	4.4%	4.8%
.1	4.0%	4.4%	4.8%	5.3%	5.9%	6.4%
.2	5.0%	5.5%	6.1%	6.7%	7.3%	8.1%
.3	3.0%	3.3%	3.6%	4.0%	4.4%	4.8%
.2	2.0%	2.2%	2.4%	2.7%	2.9%	3.2%
.1	1.0%	1.1%	1.2%	1.3%	1.5%	1.6%
.4	0.0%	0.0%	0.0%	0.0%	0.0%	0.0%
.2	3.0%	3.3%	3.6%	4.0%	4.4%	4.8%
.6	0.0%	0.0%	0.0%	0.0%	0.0%	0.0%

PROGRAM 7 - THE 10K RUN OR WALK

DISTANCE (6.2 MILES)	LEVEL 1 GRADE	LEVEL 2 GRADE	LEVEL 3 GRADE	LEVEL 4 GRADE	LEVEL 5 GRADE	LEVEL 6 GRADE
.2	0.0%	0.0%	0.0%	0.0%	0.0%	0.0%
.2	1.0%	1.1%	1.2%	1.3%	1.5%	1.6%
.4	2.0%	2.2%	2.4%	2.7%	2.9%	3.2%
.6	0.0%	0.0%	0.0%	0.0%	0.0%	0.0%
.2	1.0%	1.1%	1.2%	1.3%	1.5%	1.6%
.2	2.0%	2.2%	2.4%	2.7%	2.9%	3.2%
.2	3.0%	3.3%	3.6%	4.0%	4.4%	4.8%
.2	4.0%	4.4%	4.8%	5.3%	5.9%	6.4%
.4	5.0%	5.5%	6.1%	6.7%	7.3%	8.1%
.6	3.0%	3.3%	3.6%	4.0%	4.4%	4.8%
.4	2.0%	2.2%	2.4%	2.7%	2.9%	3.2%
.2	1.0%	1.1%	1.2%	1.3%	1.5%	1.6%
.8	0.0%	0.0%	0.0%	0.0%	0.0%	0.0%
.4	3.0%	3.3%	3.6%	4.0%	4.4%	4.8%
1.2	0.0%	0.0%	0.0%	0.0%	0.0%	0.0%

Training Suggestions. • Use the 5K and 10K programs to measure the effectiveness of your overall training program. • Don't overdo it on your first 5K or 10K! • Keep a log of your 5K and 10K times, and try to improve them as your training progresses. • If you want to do the P-6 (5K) or P-7 (10K) program without running, simply walk it! These two programs are totally appropriate for either running, walking or walk/run. • To see if you're getting better on "hill work," compare your 5K time at L1 level with your 5K time at L6 level. If your L1 and L6 times are getting closer, it means you're handling hills better. • To see if your endurance is improving, compare your 5K or 10K times at the same "L" level. If your 10K time starts to approach **twice** that of your 5K time, then your endurance is improving.

Program 8
THE PRITIKIN WORKOUT

Overview. Depending on the level you choose in the Pritikin program, you may find yourself walking (L1, L2, L3), jogging (L4, L5, L6) or running (L7, L8, L9). In either case, you'll start off with a comfortable walking warm-up before moving on to higher intensity workloads. The Pritikin P-8 strategy is to alternate between **high** and **low** intensity every minute to create an interval training effect. This helps you achieve cardiovascular conditioning, while at the same time, burning a substantial number of calories.

PRITIKIN PROGRAM	FITNESS LEVELS	MODE	MAX. PACE 1-MINUTE INTERVALS
P8	L1	walk	3.50 mph
P8	L2	walk	4.03 mph
P8	L3	walk	4.63 mph
P8	L4	jog	5.32 mph
P8	L5	jog	6.12 mph
P8	L6	jog	7.04 mph
P8	L7	run	8.10 mph
P8	L8	run	8.58 mph
P8	L9	run	9.01 mph

WHY PRITIKIN WORKOUTS WORK!

During a Pritikin P-8 workout, your muscles work anaerobically (in slight oxygen debt) for short **one-minute** bursts of activity. In the succeeding minute of moving recovery, the body shifts back into aerobic work. Now the oxygen supply in the blood has a chance to catch up to the oxygen demand of the muscles. Keep in mind that it takes the heart about **one minute** to fully catch up with an increase in workload. Therefore, in doing these **one-minute** hard intervals, your heart is never stressed beyond its maximum pumping capability. The net effect of all this is that the body learns to tolerate higher levels of lactic acid without fatiguing, and the heart and leg muscles become stronger. Also, there is an increase in the number of red blood cells, which in turn increases your oxygen carrying capacity and aerobic endurance.

SUPER TRAINING STRATEGIES

Basically, there are four directions which you can take in setting up a treadmill walking program. You can train at: (1) moderate intensity for long slow distance to **burn fat** and lose weight; (2) high-intensity for **cardiovascular** endurance; (3) alternating hard and easy intervals for improving **speed** and maximum endurance; and (4) moderate intensity for basic **health maintenance.**

Regardless of your goals, it's critical to train at workloads suitable for your level of fitness. This is easily determined by taking the 540 Supertrainer Treadmill P-1 Self-Evaluation test. Your walk-performance on this 20-minute self-evaluation will tell you whether you are Level 1 (white belt), Level 2 (yellow belt), Level 3 (orange belt), Level 4 (green belt), Level 5 (blue belt), Level 6 (purple belt), Level 7 (red belt), Level 8 (brown belt), or Level 9 (black belt).

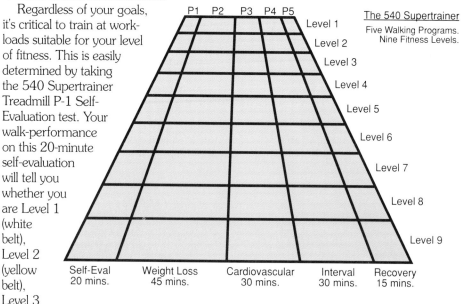

The 540 Supertrainer
Five Walking Programs.
Nine Fitness Levels.

P1 P2 P3 P4 P5 — Level 1, Level 2, Level 3, Level 4, Level 5, Level 6, Level 7, Level 8, Level 9

| Self-Eval 20 mins. | Weight Loss 45 mins. | Cardiovascular 30 mins. | Interval 30 mins. | Recovery 15 mins. |

Once establishing your fitness level, you can train using a series of computer treadmill programs specifically designed for weight loss (P2), cardiovascular conditioning (P3), speed improvement (P4) or long term maintenance and recovery (P5). Periodically re-evaluate your fitness level. Then, based on your new self-evaluation (L1,L2...L9), tune up your training program.

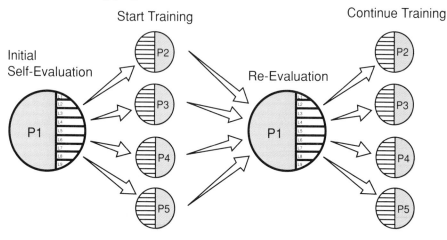

Start Training · Continue Training · Initial Self-Evaluation · Re-Evaluation · P1 · P2 · P3 · P4 · P5

The following graphs depict the walking-exercise profiles for the 540 Supertrainer computer programs.

P1 Self-Evaluation. A 20-minute test for determining your fitness level and maximum workload capacity on a treadmill.

P2 Weight Loss. A 45-minute workout designed for maximum Caloric burn at a moderate walking intensity.

P3 Cardiovascular. A 30-minute high-intensity workout for improving aerobic endurance.

P4 Interval Training. A 30-minute series of hard and easy intervals designed to increase walking speed.

P5 Recovery/Maintenance. A relatively easy 15-minute workout geared for maintenance and recovery.

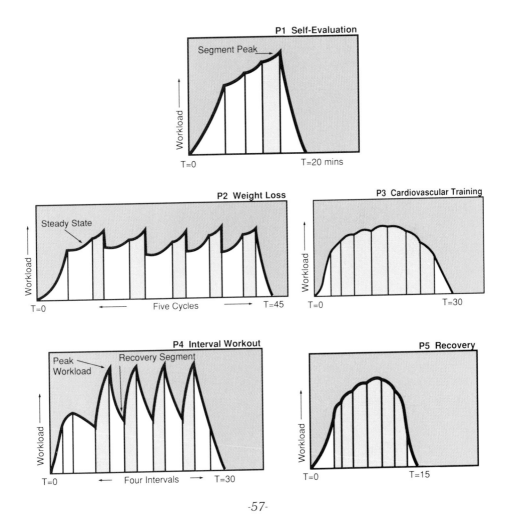

• Metabolism stays high throughout the workout. • Alternating one-minute intervals of **hard** and **easy** effort stress the body to levels it's not accustomed to – without exceeding the safe training heart rate. • User does not get bored because the speeds are always changing. • The Pritikin program can help individuals develop both their anaerobic and aerobic systems. • The Pritikin program lets the individual use a run/walk technique which can help reduce leg fatigue. • The Pritikin program provides adequate warm-up and cool-down stages, plus two extended low-intensity moving recovery intervals 17 minutes and 28 minutes into the workout. • The Pritikin program lasts a full 45 minutes, making it both a good calorie-burner and cardiovascular conditioner.

PRITIKIN, TREADMILLS
AND LONGEVITY

The Pritikin Longevity Centers turn people's lives around; they do it with diet and treadmills.

In 1976, Nathan Pritikin came to the amazing revelation that he could rehabilitate his ailing cardiovascular system through a strict regimen of diet and exercise. Soon after, his cholesterol dropped to reasonable levels and his physical energy improved significantly. Motivated by his personal lifestyle turnaround, Nathan Pritikin opened The Pritikin Longevity Center in Santa Monica, CA to help rehabilitate people from coronary heart disease and various cardiovascular disorders.

Thirteen years later, over 30,000 individuals have now "graduated" from a network of Pritikin Longevity Centers around America. Each center offers two programs (13 days and 26 days in duration) for clients who enroll. During one's stay, a battery of tests are administered (including a treadmill tolerance test and blood chemistry work ups) and educational seminars on cooking, low-fat lifestyle, exercise and stress management are given. Each person actively participates in a medically prescribed exercise program daily.

At Pritikin, the primary chosen exercise is treadmill walking because it's the most natural way a deconditioned person can do work and burn calories continuously without fatigue and muscle soreness. Currently, The Pritikin Centers own approximately 500 Trotter treadmills to support their exercise classes. This makes Pritikin the largest single user of treadmill equipment in the healthcare-fitness industry today.

The net result of all this effort is lifestyle change – not only the short-term improvements (i.e. weight loss, cholesterol lowering, aerobic improvements) seen at The Pritikin Longevity Centers, but the long-term changes people make in their lives after they leave the Pritikin learning environment. (For more information on The Pritikin Longevity Centers, call 1-800-421-9911).

Overview. The Hill-Interval program (P-9) resembles the 5K and 10K workouts (programs P-6 and P-7), but with one exception. In the P-9 program the **time** is fixed at 45 minutes, and the **distance** covered is variable. Depending on which fitness level you choose, you may be climbing hills which peak at 6% grade or 12.9% grade. The speed you choose determines the distance you'll cover during those 45 minutes. Hence, you can measure your progress by how far you go during a P-9 workout. One advantage of the P-9 program is that it gives you the freedom to set your pace based on the slope of each hill.

THE TEN TWO'S OF TREADMILL TRAINING

The Harvard Alumni research study, an investigation of the lifestyles and health histories of nearly 17,000 graduates of Harvard, led epidemiologist, Dr. Ralph Paffenbarger, to conclude that lack of physical activity is a major factor associated with heart disease. Specifically, Dr. Paffenbarger found that subjects who expended 2,000 to 3,500 Calories per week in physical activity had a significantly better chance of avoiding heart disease.

What does this translate to in the real world of treadmill walking? Try 2,000 to 2,500 Calories of treadmilling per week, **or** 200 to 250 hours of treadmilling per year **or** 22 miles of treadmilling every 2 weeks. The pay back? About 2 minutes of life extension for every minute of treadmill walking. How can you remember all this? Think of Ten Two's: 2222-222-22-2 ..... 2,222 treadmill **Calories** per week (see top row)..... 222 treadmill **hours** per year (see second row)..... 22 treadmill **miles** bi-monthly (see third row)..... 2 **minutes** more of life per minute of treadmilling.

Remembering the **Ten Two's** can help you live a longer, healthier life.

TREADMILLS PUT TIME ON YOUR SIDE

Treadmill Walking and Staying Young.
Scientific research clearly shows a positive relationship between regular physical activity and longevity. The key is consistency – staying active for life. Of all exercises, walking is the easiest to maintain over an entire lifetime. Of all forms of walking, treadmill walking is the most consistent, convenient and effective.

Walking on a treadmill helps (1) keep blood vessels more elastic; (2) speed up your metabolism; (3) slow down bone-demineralization and bone loss that cause osteoporosis; (4) maintain an erect posture by strengthening back, hip and leg muscles; (5) reduce the risk of back problems; (6) maintain muscle mass and muscle tone; (7) improve circulation to the joints; (8) increase heart volume, heart weight and cardiac output; (9) increase circulation to the skin, making "it" look smoother and healthier; and (10) normalize blood pressure.

Treadmill Training Around the Clock.
One o'clock. Two o'clock. Three o'clock. Any time of day or night is treadmill training time. Morning treadmill workouts set you up to handle the stresses of the day. Mid-day workouts increase your metabolism and control your appetite. Late afternoon and early evening treadmill walks help you unwind and "get rid of the day's hassles." Mid-evening treadmill sessions are great for creative thinking and more restful sleeps. Short treadmill sessions will help control your blood sugar levels (great for insulin dependent diabetics) and ease the tightness of arthritic joints. The bottom line...it really doesn't matter **when**... as long as you burn the **extra calories** sometime during your day – and on a **regular** basis - for life! So experiment working out at different times of the day to find out when you really enjoy treadmilling the most. That's the best time for you.

One M&M is 5 calories of sugar-coated chocolate – little ellipsoids composed of 39% fat, 55% carbohydrate and 6% protein. Not exactly a balanced meal, although children admiring the array of reds, greens, yellows and browns might disagree.

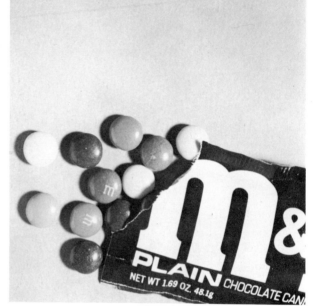

To burn off one single M&M (regardless of its color), you need to walk 48 seconds on a treadmill at 3.5 mph at 5% grade. Or, you could walk the length of a football field – end zones included.*

Not too bad. Except who eats one M&M? The small 45¢ bag holds about 50 shiny pieces, otherwise known as a handful. To burn off a bag of 50, you're talking 50 x 48 seconds of treadmill walking (2400 seconds) – commonly called a 40-minute workout.

A slice of pizza is the equivalent of 50 minutes of treadmill walking. A snip of celery…10 seconds. A large scoop of Ice Cream…60 minutes. And a Big Mac, fries and shake…four and a half hours!

*based on a 150-pound person of average metabolism.

CROSS-TRAINING WITH A TREADMILL

No matter what your sport is, treadmilling will improve it! A treadmill workout incorporates just about every muscle in the human body, including...the thighs (used in backpacking, mountain climbing, skiing and biking)...the calves, shins and hamstrings (used in running, jogging and aerobic dancing)...the torso and arms (used in golf, swimming and racquet sports).

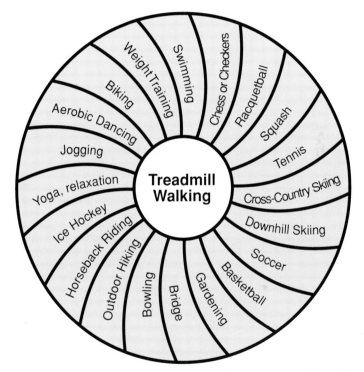

Even the brain benefits from treadmilling due to improved circulation and oxygen replenishment. Your alertness is dependent on a good supply of oxygen and the ability to remove metabolic waste products via enhanced circulation. So whether your sport or hobby is chopping trees, sailing or playing bridge, training on a treadmill should help improve your physical and mental performance.

Chapter 6

CREATIVE TREADMILLING

Sixteen treadmill exercises and games to make workouts more exciting. *

Train on a treadmill four days a week and you'll total about 200 workouts annually. Now consider, "Could you put enough variety into those 200 workouts to stay motivated?"

Interesting question. Its answer may define the longevity of your treadmill career.

So how do you maintain your excitement training on a treadmill? That's what we're about to explore – how to transform a revolving rubber mat and motor into a scenic winter wilderness, a movie plot line, a dance concert, a fitness game or a sporting event.

> *"A treadmill is a great place to think because you don't have to worry about cars or cat calls. Often, leads for new stories will pop into my head during a treadmill workout."*
>
> *Karre Slafkin,*
> *Los Angeles Freelance*
> *Writer and Editor*

First, let's start with the word: *imagination*. Treadmilling without imagination promotes boredom. As a treadmill walker, you have two choices; you can labor over the remaining minutes in your workout – or you can dream about what's over the next *mountain pass*. The former is like being a prisoner in a cell block; the latter is more like a kid exploring the countryside. You don't need to be creative to explore. You just need to be curious. Hopefully the 16 treadmill workouts which follow will help arouse the childish curiosity that is bound within you.

Workout #1
PROGRESSIVE HILLS & VALLEYS

Here's a game of *Roller Coaster* played without any downhill stretches. The idea is to climb higher and higher on a series of hills that get progressively steeper as you get deeper into your workout. The workout ends when your heart, lungs or legs say, "Enough!" Then it's time to cool down.

────────

*Note: Many of the treadmill workouts in this chapter can be fairly intense, and for that reason, they should be attempted only if you are in good health with a solid foundation of aerobic conditioning and have medical clearance from your physician.

How To Do Workout #1. Start off by walking at 0% grade on your treadmill at your normal easy warm-up pace. For most walkers this will be between 3.0 mph (20-minute mile) and 3.5 mph (17-minute mile). Warm up this way for about three to five minutes. Officially end your warm-up by raising the elevation on your treadmill by 2% (treadmill goes from 0% grade to 2% grade). Meanwhile, maintain your original pace and immediately activate your stopwatch. After walking at 2% incline for one minute, drop back to 1% grade – still holding to your original pace. One minute later, crank up the elevation by 2% grade so that you're now walking uphill at 3% grade. Hold at 3% grade for one minute; then lower the elevation back to 2% for another minute of "moving" recovery. After the minute, "leap frog" back up to 4% grade (2% increase) – and so on – 2% elevation increase followed by 1% elevation decrease.

At first this game of **progressive hills** may seem easy (i.e. walking your normal warm-up pace at 1%, 2% or even 5% grade). However, after your 12th interval, you may sing a different tune. The challenge is to see how long you can keep increasing the slope before you're forced to "quit" and start your cool-down.*

TIME	SPEED	ELEVATION
warm-up	Comfortable Pace	0% grade
1st minute	Comfortable Pace	2% grade
2nd minute	Comfortable Pace	1% grade
3rd minute	Comfortable Pace	3% grade
4th minute	Comfortable Pace	2% grade
5th minute	Comfortable Pace	4% grade
6th minute	Comfortable Pace	3% grade
7th minute	Comfortable Pace	5% grade
8th minute	Comfortable Pace	4% grade

In a **Progressive Hills** workout you're ***"taking two steps forward (2% rise in elevation) for each step backwards (1% decrease in elevation)."*** The net result is that you increase your elevation by 1% grade every two minutes. Since there is an alternating pattern of **steep** and **less steep** walking, this truly is an interval workout. **Question:** How many minutes could you last in a game of **Progressive Hills**?

———

*Note: A five to ten minute cool-down is wise to do after any workout to: (1) stabilize blood pressure, (2) return muscle tissues to a more aerobic state, and (3) flush lactic acid and carbon dioxide from the muscles before their tiny capillaries close. The latter reduces the possibilities of residual stiffness or soreness later on due to trapped metabolic waste products in the muscles.

THE *100-CALORIE WALKING RACE*

Given the freedom to walk at any **speed** or **elevation**, how fast could you walk off 100 Calories? The fitter you become, the faster you'll be able to reach the 100 Calories mark. Thus, by tracking your **100-Calorie race** times, you're really measuring improvements in your aerobic fitness. Starting tomorrow, do you think you could burn 100 Calories in 10 minutes or less? The chart below will give you some idea of your fitness level based on the time it takes you to burn off 100 Calories.

The *100-Calorie Walking Race:* How fast could you walk off 100 Calories?

FITNESS LEVEL	120-POUND* WALKER	160-POUND* WALKER	200-POUND* WALKER
Outstanding	10 minutes	8 minutes	6 minutes
Excellent	12 minutes	9 minutes	7 minutes
Very Good	14 minutes	11 minutes	9 minutes
Fair	15 minutes	12 minutes	10 minutes

---

*A Note on Scoring. In general the more you weigh the more you burn. In fact, there's a linear correlation between body weight and energy expenditure. For instance, a 200-pound man burns twice as many calories as his 100-pound wife as they walk side by side (all other factors being equal). For this reason, scoring standards are reported separately in three weight classes for workouts #2, #3, #6 and #7. Also note that the Calories spent warming up and cooling down should be excluded from the above totals.

THE 100-CALORIE RACE	DATE	TIME TO BURN 100 CALORIES
Race #1	_/_/_	__:__ (mins:secs)
Race #2	_/_/_	__:__ (mins:secs)
Race #3	_/_/_	__:__ (mins:secs)

Suggestion: For the best performances, give yourself a slow, easy warm-up prior to your 100-Calorie "Race". This will help increase blood supply and oxygen to the working muscles while allowing time for coronary arteries to dilate.

THE *200-CALORIE WALKING RACE:*

This workout is identical to the **100-Calorie Race** above, except it's twice the effort. To burn 200 Calories (instead of 100) you will need to pace yourself better and improve your cardiovascular endurance. From a conditioning standpoint, the **100-Calorie Walking Race** develops you more anaerobically; the **200-Calorie Walking Race** is better for aerobic endurance.**

**Note: High-intensity activities lasting under seven minutes are predominantly anaerobic in nature. Activities extending well beyond seven minutes tend to be more aerobic. For example, wind sprints are anaerobic; 10K races are mostly aerobic. A 1500 meter footrace is about 50% aerobic and 50% anaerobic in nature.

The 200-Calorie Walking Race: How fast can you walk off 200 calories?			
	120-POUND WALKER	**160-POUND WALKER**	**200-POUND WALKER**
Outstanding	21 minutes	17 minutes	13 minutes
Excellent	25 minutes	20 minutes	16 minutes
Very Good	29 minutes	23 minutes	19 minutes
Fair	33 minutes	25 minutes	21 minutes

THE 200-CALORIE RACE	DATE	TIME TO BURN 200 CALORIES
Race #1	__/__/__	__:__ (mins:secs)
Race #2	__/__/__	__:__ (mins:secs)
Race #3	__/__/__	__:__ (mins:secs)

Workout #4

MAXIMUM MILEAGE 6-15

Given 15 minutes, how far could you walk on a treadmill that is elevated to a 6% grade? In **Maximum Mileage 6-15** your goal is to walk as far as possible in 15 minutes. It parallels the Cooper 12-minute test, except here you're going three extra minutes up a 6% incline – all walking! As your heart muscle strengthens and your body fat drops, you should be setting new personal distance records in this 15-minute fitness game. After completing your **Maxi-Mileage 6-15** walk, compare your scores with those shown on the chart below to get a ballpark evaluation of your fitness level compared to others.

A more strenuous variation of this game is **Maximum Mileage 12-15**, in which the entire 15-minute treadmill walk is done at 12% grade instead of 6% grade.

PERFORMANCE	MAXIMUM MILEAGE 6-15 6% FOR 15 MINUTES	MAXIMUM MILEAGE 12-15 12% FOR 15 MINUTES
Outstanding	1.40 miles	1.25 miles
Excellent	1.20 miles	1.05 miles
Very Good	1.00 miles	0.85 miles
Fair	0.80 miles	0.65 miles
Enter your distance	___ miles	___ miles

If you could walk 1.2 miles up a 6% grade in 15 minutes, could you double that distance in 30 minutes? Maybe – depending on your cardiovascular endurance. After a **Maximum Mileage 6-30** workout, you'll know for sure.

Objective: Walk as far as possible in 30 minutes @ 6% (or 12%) elevation.

PERFORMANCE	MAXIMUM MILEAGE 6-30 6% FOR 30 MINUTES	MAXIMUM MILEAGE 12-30 12% FOR 30 MINUTES
Outstanding	2.7 miles	2.4 miles
Excellent	2.3 miles	2.0 miles
Very Good	1.9 miles	1.6 miles
Fair	1.5 miles	1.2 miles
Enter your distance	__ miles	__ miles

The challenge of **MaxiCal-15** is to **burn as many calories as possible in 15 minutes of treadmill walking**. You can set the treadmill speed **as fast as** you want, or increase the elevation **as high as** you can tolerate. But remember, the goal is to do the most work in 15 minutes. **Hint:** In MaxiCal-15 it helps to thoroughly warm up before launching into your maximum effort.

ATTEMPT	MAXIMUM CALORIES 15 MINUTES
#1	____
#2	____
#3	____

In **MaxiCal-30** the previously described workout is extended to **30 full** minutes, making it an even better endurance challenge.

Attempt	Maximum Calories 30 Minutes
#1	___
#2	___
#3	___

MaxiCal Performance	Weight 120 Pounds	Weight 160 Pounds	Weight 200 Pounds
Excellent	120 calories*	160 calories*	200 calories*
	230 calories**	300 calories**	380 calories**
Very Good	110 calories*	145 calories*	180 calories*
	200 calories**	270 calories**	340 calories**

*for MaxiCal 15 **for MaxiCal 30

Workout #8
How High Can You Climb?

Ever wonder how high you climb during a hard treadmill workout? For example, if you walked 30 minutes at 3 mph at a 10% grade, you would cover a distance of 1.5 miles or 7920 horizontal feet. Since you climb one foot vertically for every 10 feet covered on a 10% grade, your 7920-foot walk translates to a vertical lift of 792 feet – a small ski slope. To climb the equivalent of Mt. McKinley (Elev. 20,320), you'd have to walk 203,200 feet on a treadmill at a 10% grade. That's 38.5 miles! Not an unreasonable goal for two months of training. If Mt. McKinley is a bit too high for you, set your sights on some lower peaks...

Mountain	Vertical Climb (ft)	Treadmill Equivalency
Savage Mountain	2,850	5.4 miles @ 10% grade
Terrible Mountain	2,884	5.5 miles @ 10% grade
Killington Peak	4,235	8.0 miles @ 10% grade
Mt. Washington	6,288	11.9 miles @ 10% grade
Lost Trail Pass	7,410	14.0 miles @ 10% grade
Elk Calf Mountain	7,610	14.4 miles @ 10% grade

Mountain	Vertical Climb (ft)	Treadmill Equivalency
Mt. St. Helen's	8,365	15.8 miles @ 10% grade
Mt. Garibaldi (Can)	8,787	16.6 miles @ 10% grade
Mt. Hood	11,239	21.3 miles @ 10% grade
Hole in the Mtn. Peak	11,276	21.4 miles @ 10% grade
Mauna Kee (Hawaii)	13,796	26.1 miles @ 10% grade
Mt. Shasta	14,162	26.8 miles @ 10% grade
Mt. Ranier	14,410	27.3 miles @ 10% grade
Mt. McKinley	20,320	38.5 miles @ 10% grade

Example: In a recent 60-minute treadmill workout, Sally walked 30 minutes at 3 mph on a 5% grade and the other 30 minutes at 4.0 mph on an 8% grade. How high did she climb during her workout?

To calculate Sally's total climb, break her workout into two segments: (1) her 5% climb and (2) her 8% climb.

Climb at 5% grade = 0.50 hour x 3.0 mph x 5280'/mile x 0.05 = 396'
Climb at 8% grade = 0.50 hour x 4.0 mph x 5280'/mile x 0.08 = 844'
Total Vertical Climb = 1240 feet

FOR EACH MILE WALKED YOU CAN CLAIM THE FOLLOWING VERTICAL CLIMBS AT THE % GRADE SHOWN BELOW

0.0% grade	0 feet
0.1% grade	5 feet
0.5% grade	26 feet
1.0% grade	53 feet
2.0% grade	106 feet
3.0% grade	158 feet
4.0% grade	211 feet
5.0% grade	264 feet
6.0% grade	317 feet
7.0% grade	370 feet
8.0% grade	422 feet
9.0% grade	475 feet
10.0% grade	528 feet
11.0% grade	581 feet
12.0% grade	634 feet
13.0% grade	686 feet
14.0% grade	739 feet
15.0% grade	792 feet

First set your treadmill at a reasonable walking elevation – perhaps between 5% and 10% grade. Next, begin walking at a comfortable warm-up pace; then gradually start increasing your pace in accordance with how you feel (elevation is constant). Walk as long as your endurance will reasonably take you. Then cool down.

At the conclusion of your workout, note your mileage. Then, using the mileage-elevation conversion tables, calculate your **vertical climb.** As your training progresses, try "climbing to new heights" on single workouts. Or try to climb your favorite mountain in a record-breaking number of days. If you're into real mountain climbing and backpacking, **The Big Treadmill Climb** workout will enhance your endurance at higher altitudes.*

Workout #10
S&E INTERVALS

S&E is a workout consisting of alternating intervals during which the **speed** and **elevation** take turns increasing individually by a fixed amount every minute. Regardless of your ability, begin walking at 2.5 mph at 0% elevation for your first **S&E** minute (warm-up). A minute later, increase the speed to 2.6 miles per hour at 0% elevation. At T=two minutes, increase the elevation to 1%, without changing the speed. The next minute the speed increases 0.1 mph (to 2.7 mph). This pattern continues such that after each minute there is an alternate increase in **speed** or **elevation** (0.1 mph or 1% grade, respectively). Your goal is to stay on the treadmill as long as is comfortably possible.

ELAPSED TIME	SPEED (MPH)	TREADMILL ELEVATION
0	2.5	0%
1	2.6	0%
2	2.6	1%
3	2.7	1%
4	2.7	2%
5	2.8	2%
6	2.8	3%
7	2.9	3%
8	2.9	4%
9	3.0	4%

Question. *If you tried the* **S&E Interval** *workout today, could you last 20 minutes? How about 25 or 30 minutes?*

Note: *The longer you stay on this protocol, the fitter you are becoming.*

Note: In climbing at altitudes greater than 5000 feet, you may experience oxygen deficiencies leading to shortness of breath, dizziness, premature fatigue and sleepiness. Realize that there is about a one percent drop in your aerobic capacity for each 1000 feet you rise above 5000-foot elevation. The best ways to prepare for high-altitude hiking are to do: (1) interval-type (treadmill) workouts which increase oxygen carrying capacity; (2) leg strengthening exercises such as backwards uphill walking; and (3) general aerobic conditioning. Also, don't forget to acclimate gradually on arriving at a new altitude zone. This is best accomplished by not exercising vigorously for one or two days.

Workout #11
THE ONE-MILE HILL SPRINT

The object here is to *sprint* one mile uphill at a 5% grade. Set your treadmill at a 5% elevation and walk straight uphill until 1.00 miles appears on your display panel. Because this is a fairly vigorous workout, warm-up extra carefully prior to *charging* up this hill. Also, hold back a bit at the start to prevent your calf muscles, Achilles tendons and shins from tightening up when they are relatively cold and inflexible.

Workout #12
THE MOUNTAIN MILE

Workout #12 is almost identical to **The One-Mile Hill Sprint**, except the hill (5% grade) is now a mountain (10% grade). In doing workouts 11 and 12, you might compare your best times for climbing both the **mountain** and the **hill**. If you could walk the 5% hill in 15 minutes (4 mph pace...adjusted workload of 4.5 mph), then you should be able to climb the mountain in 17 minutes (3.5 mph pace...adjusted workload of 4.5 mph). If not, your thighs and calves may need more toning at lower workloads.

CLIMBING HILLS (5%) AND MOUNTAINS (10%)

	YOUR 1-MILE TIME	AVERAGE PACE	AVERAGE SPEED
Hill Climb (5% grade)	___	___	___
Mountain Climb (10% grade)	___	___	___

Workout #13
WALK-RUN FARTLEKS

If you want to mix a little running in with your walking, or vice versa, consider **Fartlek** training. The word **Fartlek** is of Swedish origin, translating to speed play. Taken in its broadest sense, a Fartlek workout is one in which the style, speed, terrain and intensity are varied to help you enjoy the training more.

Treadmill **Fartleks** are a series of mini-workouts linked together into one consecutive training session. For instance, a 30-minute walk can be sub-divided into three 10-minute legs of varying intensities.

FARTLEK TRAINING	10 minutes Moderate Pace	10 minutes Faster Pace	10 minutes Slower Pace

Alternating treadmill running and treadmill walking is another type of **Fartlek** training. On a treadmill, the **run-walk** or **walk-run** possibilities are endless.

Walk-Run Intervals of Equal Time Proportion
Walk two minutes…run two minutes…walk two… run two…walk two…run two…walk two…etc.

Walk-Run Intervals of Unequal Proportion
Walk three minutes…run one minute…walk three… run one…walk three…run one…etc.

Walk-Run Fastest 5K
Give yourself alternating two-minute walking and running intervals at a constant grade of say 5%, and see how fast you can cover 3.1 miles (5K).

Walk-Run 500 Calories
Start out walking at a comfortable pace and elevation. On hitting 50 Calories, start jogging. At 100 calories, switch back to walking…and so on… until reaching 500 Calories. Then cool down and record your time for 500 Calories.

Walk-Run a TV Show
In the span of a half hour TV show, time your walking and running intervals such that you **walk** during the program and **run** during the commercials. For fun and fitness, see how many **calories** you can accumulate for different TV shows.

Workout #14
NEWSPAPER TREADMILLING

Warning: This workout is to be done at your own risk. It involves reading on a treadmill which can upset your balance – especially if you're not extremely careful and adept in your footwork.

One of the most unhealthy walks in American lifestyle is the one from the dinner table to the Lazy Boy. Average distance: ten yards. Average caloric burn: one calorie – and that's being generous. Fall asleep reading the newspaper, and you're on your way to wearing dinner around your waist.

However, if you walked from the dinner table to your treadmill with a newspaper in hand, you could start a 400-Calorie reading which will fill your mind and flatten your stomach. It's amazing how a few interesting news stories can make treadmill minutes fly by.

Note: To be a successful reader on the treadmill, you must learn to walk tall and stay centered on the treadmill belt. It also helps to walk slower on a steeper incline to keep your balance while driving up your heart rate. However, never push hard after a meal because your cardiorespiratory system is competing with your digestive system for blood flow and oxygen.

Workout #15
TREADMILLING TO MUSIC

Did you ever hear of a five-song workout? If not, put on a headset and dial in your favorite FM radio station. Use the opening song for a warm-up; then increase speed and elevation as the songs pick up in tempo. Hold a steady pace through commercials and the news, and then try to crank up the intensity as the beat continues. Some FM stations play five songs in 18 minutes; if that's not long enough for you, stay on the treadmill for a few extra requests.

> *"Right after work, I'm usually stressed out to the max. To come back down, I set up musical tapes alongside the treadmill. I try to match the tapes to my mood. It's a kind of therapy. They call it* **iso-moodic therapy**. *For example, if I'm all hyper, I'll start my (treadmill) workout with some jazzy Rock 'n Roll, something like a Hendrix or Rolling Stone cut. Later on into my workout, the music usually starts to mellow out with some Crosby, Stills and Nash or some folksy stuff. By my cool-down, the sounds are smooth and so am I."*

> Wayne McCarty
> General Manager, Carolina Fitness
> **Aug. 1988:** 210 pounds & stressed
> **Sept. 1988:** Started treadmill training
> **Feb. 1989:** 185 pounds & still going
> **Hobby:** Musical Treadmilling

Warning: Wearing headsets outside on streets and highways can be hazardous to your health. One Washington runner learned his lesson the hard way as a vehicle (he never heard) struck him from behind. Now he's paralyzed from the waist down. Fortunately for you, there shouldn't be any motor vehicles running through your exercise room.

TELEPHONE TREADMILLING:
TALK-AND-TRAIN

Most of us spend enough time on the telephone each day to have three or four good workouts. If just one of your telephone conversations was converted to a treadmill workout, you wouldn't have to sacrifice any extra time for training. So why not **talk-and-train** simultaneously? As long as you're walking aerobically, you should be able to carry on a conversation freely, even if you do sound a little strange breathing heavily into the other end of the line.

TWENTY-THREE WAYS TO
KILL TIME ON A TREADMILL

*Here are some things to think about and do to pass time on a treadmill...*Picture yourself five pounds lighter....Dream about your ideal vacation....Watch a video movie **(Gone With The Wind** is worth 1500 Calories)....Focus on your determined look in the mirror....Think how you'll re-arrange your treadmill exercise room....Recall the highlights of this past year in your life....Think about the kind of work you'd really like to do....Dream up a new business....Watch a sporting event on TV....Listen to talk radio (Larry King trains on a treadmill)....Tune into your favorite music with a headset....Meditate by staring at an object straight ahead of you....Watch the wind blow trees outside....Invite friends over for a treadmill party (5-minute turns)....Recall your funniest dates....Record your feelings on a tape recorder....Call up a friend with a treadmill and workout together....Read a book, magazine or newspaper....Play a book on a cassette **(Blue Highways** is five great hours of treadmilling)....Play the games outlined in this chapter....Compose a poem....Count the number of footsteps you take in a minute....Compose the opening of a letter to a distant friend.

CREATIVE TREADMILLING SUMMARY

WORKOUT NAME	DESCRIPTION OF WORKOUT	KEEPING SCORE
1. Progressive Hills & Valleys	Walk a series of steeper & steeper hills.	Record how long you were able to sustain the workout.
2. The 100-Calorie Walking Race	Walk off 100 calories ASAP.	Record the time it took you to burn 100 Calories.
3. The 200-Calorie Walking Race	Walk off 200 calories ASAP.	Record your 200-Calorie time.
4. Maxi Mileage 6-15	At 6% elevation, walk as far as possible in 15 minutes?	Record your mileage.
5. Maxi Mileage 6-30	At 6% elevation, walk as far as possible in 30 minutes?	Record your mileage.
6. MaxiCal 15	15 minutes of treadmill walking for maximum calories!	Record your calories for 15 minutes of walking.
7. MaxiCal 30	30 minutes of treadmill walking for maximum calories!	Record your calories for 30 minutes of walking.
8. How High Can You Climb?	Climb your favorite mountain in "x" days.	Record your vertical climbs.
9. The Big Climb	Go for your maximum climb in one treadmill session.	Record your vertical climb per session.
10. S&E Intervals	Alternate speed and elevation increases in one-minute intervals.	Record the number of minutes you were able to last.
11. The One-Mile Hill Sprint	How fast can you walk one mile on a 5% grade?	Record your pace and time for the mile.
12. The Mountain Mile	How fast can you walk one mile on a 10% grade?"	Record your pace and time for the mile.
13. Walk-Run Fartleks	A walk-run-walk-run form of interval training.	Record your Walk-Run ratio
14. Newspaper Treadmilling	Burning off dinner instead of crashing in the Lazy Boy.	Clip interesting articles from the newspaper.
15. Treadmilling to Music	Bopping to the beat on a treadmill.	Note which FM stations give you your best training workouts.
16 Telephone Talk-and-Train	Telephone talk and an aerobic high all at once.	Record total calories and your telephone time.

Chapter 7

PROGRESSIVE TREADMILLING

Training strategies to last you a lifetime.

After a year of treadmill training, Jackie increased her speed from 3 mph @ 3% grade to 4 mph @ 8% grade. At first she was thrilled with her progress. But lately her enthusiasm and drive have fallen as she has found it increasingly more difficult to improve. It was as if her body had reached its potential – and there was nothing left to train for. Subsequently, her training slipped and her weight kept creeping up. Then one day she woke up, looked in the mirror and said, "My lord, I've got to get back onto my treadmill."

Jackie's story is the Catch 22 of fitness walking! The fitter you become, the tougher it gets to improve. A deconditioned person starting on a treadmill walking program often sees initial rapid gains, including reductions in weight and body fat, and improvements in endurance, energy and muscle tone.

A very fit person however, can train ever harder while hardly improving at all. It seems unfair, working out for little visible gain. It's a classic case of the law of diminishing returns. Experiencing this can be demotivating. Individuals who keep pushing harder can even self-destruct.

"The perfect treadmill workout is the one that motivates you to do it again a day later."

> Peter Haines,
> President of Trotter
> and Treadmill Walker

The key to long-term survival is understanding and accepting your body for what it is – setting goals based on **maintenance** and **good health,** not on just improving or setting new records. It's important to realize that **maintenance** is **progress** too. If you hold your own against **time** and **the aging process,** you're a winner.

Our prime objective should be to maintain our health and mobility over the next 30 or 40 years. That's progress! This point can be better appreciated when you stop to consider that your: (1) body loses approximately 10% of its muscle mass per decade, (2) maximum heart rate decreases by about one beat per minute per year, (3) muscle flexibility drops about 10% per decade, (4) metabolism slows down significantly starting around 30 to 35 years of age, and (5) blood vessels lose elasticity with time (hardening of the arteries).

Aging can be a depressing subject. However, if you train with preservation in mind, holding your own can be inspiring! That's why hitting a plateau in a treadmill program is O.K. The trick is to keep the excitement going when your body is near its full physical potential. Following are 11 sensible rules to follow to maintain a **progressive**, lifelong treadmill program. Read them. Discuss them with friends. Try putting them into practice!

1. Work From a Baseline. Know thyself! From the very start of your treadmill walking program, evaluate your aerobic capacity. This can be as simple as taking a 20-minute self-evaluation test, measuring your resting heart rate and blood pressure, or seeing how far you can walk in 15 consecutive minutes. These measurements will at least quantify your current physical condition.

2. Set Specific Goals. What do you want to achieve? Greater cardiovascular endurance? More energy? Less body fat? Lower blood pressure? Stress relief? Basic maintenance and long-term health? Think about it; then write down your specific goals and a plan to accomplish them.

3. Pick a Consistent Time. The time of day you exercise doesn't really matter as long as it satisfies you. If you can train regularly at one particular time – and you enjoy working out then – that's your ideal time. The best way to find your **ideal training time** is by *trial-and-error.* Try working out in the early morning, mid-day, late afternoon and evening, and see when your body and mind enjoy it the most.

"During pregnancy, my obstetrician recommended that I walk instead of run. So I switched to brisk walking on a treadmill. As a result, I kept my weight under control right up through my delivery without complications. Now I train on a treadmill after work to relieve tension and to curb my appetite."

Brenda Atherton,
Mother and Vice President
of General Recreation Corp.
Atlanta, GA

4. Build Gradually. Fools rush in and fools burn out. If you're starting a treadmill program, shoot for small incremental gains. For example, if you increased your treadmill walks by one **minute** a week, you'd be training at 52 minutes per day within a year of starting your program. How many treadmill walkers do you know that average 52 minutes per day?

5. Keep a Log. Twenty minutes after an experience, the human mind remembers about 50% of what it saw. If you train without recording your accomplishments, your progress will evaporate into the sky. If you write "it" down, you'll have it forever (see Chapter 8).

6. Cross-Train Your Muscles. Even if treadmill walking was the best exercise in the world, it would pay to diversify your training for a balanced mind and balanced body. Consider: **Swimming:** upper body muscle tone. **Static stretching:** overall muscle flexibility. **Massage:** muscle relaxation and improved circulation. **Bicycling:** thighs and calves. **Sit-ups:** abdominal strength. **Weight training:** overall strength and muscular endurance. **Hiking:** leg tone, weight control, relaxation and creativity.

7. Listen to Your Body. Your body has a lot to say! It gives you warning signs such as sore knees, stiff backs, fatigue, tight muscles, plus mood changes. These are your cues for backing off. Ignore them and you're headed for a crash landing. These are all part of what is commonly referred to as the overuse syndrome. They indicate that you've gone too far, too soon, too fast.

8. Be Open Minded to Change. The older we get, the more we come to realize how little we really know. Every day we can gain new training insights by being open-minded, by listening to others, and by trying new training techniques. Our training stagnates the minute we close our minds to new suggestions.

9. Appreciate the Little Changes. *Little changes* make the *big differences.* You don't have to step up one whole level (say from L4 to L5) to make real progress. Just being able to work out one minute longer is good progress. Even from a qualitative standpoint, appreciate the subtle changes in your moods, stress levels and energy resulting from your training. It's the sum of all these *little* improvements that makes the *big* difference.

10. Reward Systems. When you've worked hard and achieved a goal, reward yourself. Take yourself out to a great dinner. Buy yourself some new training clothes. Take a short vacation – maybe bed-and-breakfast style away from it all.

11. Be Happy, Be Realistic. Whatever you do, however you train, be happy at it. Survey yourself in the mirror and take stock of who you really are. Then, be yourself! Realizing you're not going to be the next Olympic gold medalist in the marathon can relieve the tension in your workouts. It enables you to be a kid again, to have fun, to play on the treadmill.

THE THEORIES OF TRAINING PROGRESSION
A decade in the life of an amateur athlete; training theories that do and don't work!

The idea is to get fit and stay fit. Or, is it to keep getting fitter until you breakdown from injury? Wait a minute! Isn't getting fit supposed to be healthy? If so, why do so many fitness enthusiasts drop out of training? The theories of training (described next) may help keep your treadmill program alive.**

The "Yo-Yo" Theory. People who live by the "Yo-Yo" theory of training live in fanatic cycles – whether it be to lose 20 pounds or to train for a competitive race. For example, a runner goes wild training intensely for three months, just to prepare for a marathon. The event comes – he does well and then drops out of training to catch up

---

Note: Throughout this chapter we have avoided using the word **adherence or **compliance** in talking about fitness training, and for one good reason – these words connote something akin to a jail sentence – a dose of doctor's medicine you need to swallow each day. By their very nature, these words are a complete turn off! Most of us would rather hear and talk about the positive side of persistent training inspired by wanting to exercise, and not be told that we need to adhere or comply with some dosage of daily exercise.

on all the TV and desserts he's missed for the last three months. His weight goes back up 15 pounds. By spring he's eyeing another marathon, preparing to take on another crash training program. So the cycle goes...three months on, three months off. The problem comes when he loses his appetite for that next race.

The "PR" Theory. This is also known as **The Speeding Train Crash** theory in which your goal in fitness training is to keep setting new Personal Records (PR's): faster miles...longer runs...faster longer runs. There's always some goal out there to shoot for – and the purpose of training is to give you the capacity to do that "4-minute mile." **Point to Consider:** The natural aging process will ultimately limit your physical capacity to set new personal bests. You must accept the small declines that all athletes experience as they age.

The Follow-the-Crowd Theory. Everyone's been jogging or bouncing on an aerobics dance floor, so why not do it yourself? It's the "in thing" to do – and you don't want to be left out of the social fitness scene. So you buy new shoes and a warm-up suit, a walkman and a headband and jump right in – even though "it" (the exercise) doesn't feel all that great. **Point to Consider:** Wouldn't you really rather be doing something you truly enjoy – something that makes your body feel good and not sore?

The Ice Cream Training Theory. Remember there's a double scoop of Rocky Road right over that final hill. Just finish your 10K workout, shower and give your body that special treat it trained so hard to deserve. **Point to Consider:** Does a 400-calorie workout deserve a 400-calorie treat? Think about fat, cholesterol, and all those people who claim to exercise but never seem to lose weight! Wonder why?

Seasonal Training. Everyone likes firm thighs, buttocks and a flat stomach for the beach. So what if you wear a few extra pounds, playing like Santa at Christmas. It's your winter coat of fat! It's no wonder so many training programs kick-off after New Year's Day, and fade by late fall, just in time for turkey, egg nog and the NFL playoffs. **Point to Consider:** One of the best advantages of having a treadmill in your home is to train 12 months instead of six.

The "I've-Been-There" Theory. You were a college track star and marched in the Armed Forces; you've done enough walking in your day to last a lifetime. Now it's time to sit back, take it easy and enjoy life. You earned it! **Point to Consider:** People forced into army-type, basic-training drills often learn to despise "training" later in life. Unfortunately, research shows you can't "bank" or "store up" your training benefits. The minute you become inactive, your vulnerability to heart disease increases. What really counts is your **current state** of physical activity!

Go For 2% A Week! How fast should you progress in your treadmill walking program? Some physiologists say 2% a week. That doesn't sound like much, but think about it! After 52 weeks, you'd have more than doubled your training – without shocking your system with abrupt step changes! **Point to Consider:** On paper, 2% a week sounds great! But who has the patience to creep this slowly? Most of us want to progress faster than going from 1.00 miles to 1.02 miles in a week's time. What kind of progression would satisfy you?

The Pleasure Theory of Training. You walk outdoors some days and indoors on others, just to "feel good." You don't care about being super fit; you train on a treadmill just because it sets you up for a natural high for the rest of the day. **Point to Consider:** If you're not enjoying your training workouts, you're going to have a problem down the road.

> "When I'm having trouble getting motivated to get on the treadmill, I just remind myself how good I'll feel after the workout. That's enough to get me going."
>
> John Graner
> Studio City, CA

The "One-Minute-Only" Theory. If you're having trouble convincing yourself to start a walking program, commit to one minute today! Tomorrow, tack on one extra minute. Each day thereafter, just keep adding one little extra minute. After all, what's a minute? If you kept doing this for a year, you'd reach 365 minutes of walking per day (6 hours a day) within a year. **Point to Consider:** If you added just a few seconds a day to your treadmill walking – and kept it up consistently – you'd have one of the most vigorous training programs possible by the year's end.

The 540 Supertrainer Progression. The 540 Supertrainer treadmill progression starts with the P-1 Self-Evaluation Test to classify your fitness level (L1, L2, ...L9). Next, you select training programs consistent with your goals (P-2 for weight loss, P-3 for cardiovascular endurance, etc.). After months of training, re-take the P-1 Self-Evaluation. Your new score will tell if you've advanced, regressed, or stayed on the same fitness level. Then, resume training at your new fitness level. **Point to Consider:** What do you think your current "L" level is? How long would it take you to jump up one level on the "L" fitness ladder?

HOW FIT ARE YOU FOR YOUR AGE?

Progress cannot always be measured in absolute terms. Your age is a major factor in training which must be taken into account. For example, if you trained religiously for 15 years on a treadmill, only to see your fitness level drop from L6 to L5, you might get discouraged. However, by using a very simple **Age-Adjusted** formula, you can estimate your personal fitness based on your age. We call this term FITNESS AGE SCORE (FAS) as defined by the equation:

FAS = 40L + 4(A-40)

Where "L" is your fitness level as determined in your P-1 Self-Evaluation; "A" is your age. Once you calculate your **FAS,** checkout your fitness classification on the following chart (Note: In the **FAS** equation, use L=30 even if you have yet to reach that age).

FAS (FITNESS AGE SCORE)	MEN'S FITNESS CLASSIFICATION		WOMEN'S FITNESS CLASSIFICATION	
360 and above	A+	(super)	A++	(super-super)
320 and above	A	(outstanding)	A+	(super)
280 and above	A-	(excellent)	A	(outstanding)
240 and above	B+	(very good)	A-	(excellent)
200 and above	B	(good)	B+	(very good)
160 and above	B-	(fair)	B	(good)
130 and above	C	(below avg)	B-	(fair)
110 and above	D	(poor)	C	(below avg)

Example 1. At age 55, Harry scored **L5** on his P-1 Self-Evaluation. Five years later at age 60, after a consistent half decade of treadmill walking, he took his P-1 Self-Test only to find his fitness level still at L5. **Question:** Should Harry be satisfied?

$$FAS_{55} = 40L + 4(55-40)$$
$$= 40(5) + 4(55-40)$$
$$= 260 \text{ (B+, very good)}$$

$$FAS_{60} = 40(5) + 4(60-40)$$
$$= 200 + 80$$
$$= 280 \text{ (A-, excellent)}$$

Answer. At first it appears that five years of treadmill training have netted Harry a **zero** gain. Yet if he had done nothing for those five years, his "L" level would probably have been much lower. The fact that Harry maintained an L5 fitness level is a positive sign. This is reflected in his **FAS** which went from 260 to 280. It means that he has offset the aging processes that are acutely apparent in his more sedentary peers. Harry is able to do things physically that his friends cannot. What will your **FAS** be when you turn 75?

THE IMPORTANCE OF ROLE MODELING

For a moment, put aside all the theories and papers speculating why people do or don't stick to their exercise programs. Reading through such articles can bore you to sleep and even contribute to your lack of exercise adherence. Often it seems as if a group of sports behavioral scientists and doctors have adopted the 10 most accepted laws of human nature and sociology to explain exercise compliance. Unfortunately, they always overlook the biggest factor: **ROLE MODELING.**

Behind every long-term success story, there's a role model. Role models don't **tell.** They **show.** Their acts are living testimonies to their beliefs. Role models talk from their heart; not from a research podium. They earn respect by their actions. They are real.

Your role model is your invisible workout partner. He or she is always there, through the hard times, when your training is faltering. Sometimes we let our role models watch us on the sidelines. Other times, we dream about reaching their achievements.

Take the case of the little boy Ed Lamb, who in 1910 at age seven, ran alongside the railroad tracks in Toledo, Ohio, trying to catch the famous pedestrian, Edward Payson Weston. Weston was then walking across America at age 71. Somehow Lamb got through the crowds and shook Weston's hand.

Weston, at age 22, once recieved inspiration when Abraham Lincoln greeted Weston with a congratulatory handshake for walking 453 miles in 10 plus days. That was 1861 when Weston walked from Boston to Washington D.C. to hear Abraham Lincoln's inaugural speech.

In 1984, 74 years after Lamb and Weston met, I found Mr. Lamb (81) walking in Toledo, Ohio. I walked up to him and shook his hand. The octagenarian looked at me with a twinkle in his eyes and replied, "You just shook hands with the man who shook the hand of the man who shook hands with Abraham Lincoln."

Chapter 8

KEEPING SCORE
Tracking Treadmill Miles;
The Treadmill Training Log-Chart.

Keeping a training log takes commitment – something many of us seem to lose after a hard, sweaty treadmill workout. When we're looking ahead to a refreshing shower, who has time to sit down and write notes about a workout? After all, the workout is complete! Yet, without keeping records our efforts are soon forgotten. Can you recall specific details of your training program from a year ago?

What we're talking about is one minute a day! That's about all it takes to record a few simple facts about our training workouts. Then we'd all have something to look back on in life – an accurate measure of where we've been, where we're at and where we're headed. A training journal brings the past, present and future together to help keep our motivation alive.

> "I record all my workouts. I always say,
> **'Winners keep records.'"**
>
> John Graner,
> Treadmill Walker

The question is, "How can **Keeping Score** be made simple, quick, meaningful and motivating?" In the next few pages you'll discover how a new **Treadmill Training Log-Chart** can turn you into a great scorekeeper.

TREADMILL TRAINING LOGS

How long would it take you to write down the *time, distance* and *calories* covered in one treadmill workout? Half of a minute...maybe a minute. Can you afford one minute for the 45 minutes you've invested in training? Before you answer, turn to the **Treadmill Training Log-Chart** and examine the simplicity of this record keeping system.

First, note that one **Treadmill Training Log-Chart** covers **four** weeks of training. For each of the 28 days in this four-week period, you are given a box to write in. The box contains three parameters: **miles, minutes** and **calories**. The **Calorie** is the critical variable because it reflects your true total workload.

For example, compare walking one mile in 20 minutes at 0% grade to walking that same distance in 20 minutes at 15% grade. On paper, both workouts would get recorded as one mile. In reality however, a 160-pound person spends **85 Calories** walking a 20-minute mile at **0% grade** (about four Calories per minute) and **200 Calories** walking that same mile at **15% grade** (10 Calories per minute). Conclusion: **miles** don't tell the whole story on a treadmill.

The key factor is total workload as measured in **Calories**. Total Calories per workout take everything into account: your weight, the treadmill speed, the percent elevation and the distance you covered.

THE CALORIE-PER-MINUTE INTENSITY SCALE.

The two simplest ways to measure the intensity of your workout are to: (1) check your heart rate and (2) calculate your **Average Calories Per Minute (CPM)**. The higher your **CPM**, the more intense your treadmill workout. To find your **CPM** for any given workout, divide your **total treadmill Calories** by your **total workout time**. The **Workout Intensity** chart below can then be used to evaluate your relative workout intensity. With experience, you'll soon develop a natural feel for appreciating the difference between 8, 10 and 12 CPM workouts.

CALORIES PER MINUTE (CPM)			
INTENSITY OF TREADMILL WALKING	**WEIGHING 120 POUNDS**	**WEIGHING 160 POUNDS**	**WEIGHING 200 POUNDS**
Very High	above 9	above 12	above 15
High	7 to 9	10 to 12	12 to 15
Medium	5 to 7	7 to 10	9 to 12
Low	below 5	below 7	below 9

SETTING GOALS

After using the **Treadmill Training Log** for a month, you'll probably discover trends in your training. Hopefully this will inspire you to set some goals. Consider for example: (1) setting a goal to increase your training intensity by shooting for higher **CPM** workouts and higher **CPM averages** for your 28-day periods; (2) keeping tabs on your training consistency by totaling all the days within a 28-day period on which you worked out. If you divided that number by 28 and multiplied the quotient by 100, you'd arrive at your **Treadmill Consistency Factor** (TCF). For example, if your trained 21 out of 28 days, your **TCF** would be 75%; (3) monitor your **total treadmill calories** for the 28-day period and aim for higher energy expenditures; (4) measure and record your vital signs monthly. You may see **reductions** in your resting heart rate, blood pressure, serum cholesterol, body weight and percent body fat.

	WEEK #	WEEK #	WEEK #	WEEK #	TREADMILL TRAINING LOG CHART
MON	MILES ☐ MINS. ☐ CALS. ☐	MILES ☐ MINS. ☐ CALS. ☐	MILES ☐ MINS. ☐ CALS. ☐	MILES ☐ MINS. ☐ CALS. ☐	
TUE	MILES ☐ MINS. ☐ CALS. ☐	MILES ☐ MINS. ☐ CALS. ☐	MILES ☐ MINS. ☐ CALS. ☐	MILES ☐ MINS. ☐ CALS. ☐	
WED	MILES ☐ MINS. ☐ CALS. ☐	MILES ☐ MINS. ☐ CALS. ☐	MILES ☐ MINS. ☐ CALS. ☐	MILES ☐ MINS. ☐ CALS. ☐	
THU	MILES ☐ MINS. ☐ CALS. ☐	MILES ☐ MINS. ☐ CALS. ☐	MILES ☐ MINS. ☐ CALS. ☐	MILES ☐ MINS. ☐ CALS. ☐	
FRI	MILES ☐ MINS. ☐ CALS. ☐	MILES ☐ MINS. ☐ CALS. ☐	MILES ☐ MINS. ☐ CALS. ☐	MILES ☐ MINS. ☐ CALS. ☐	
SAT	MILES ☐ MINS. ☐ CALS. ☐	MILES ☐ MINS. ☐ CALS. ☐	MILES ☐ MINS. ☐ CALS. ☐	MILES ☐ MINS. ☐ CALS. ☐	**YEAR TO DATE** MILES ☐
SUN	MILES ☐ MINS. ☐ CALS. ☐	MILES ☐ MINS. ☐ CALS. ☐	MILES ☐ MINS. ☐ CALS. ☐	MILES ☐ MINS. ☐ CALS. ☐	MINS. ☐ CALS. ☐ AVG. $\frac{CAL}{MIN}$ ☐
WEEK # TOTALS	MILES ☐ MINS. ☐ CALS. ☐ AVG. $\frac{CAL}{MIN}$ ☐	**WEEK # TOTALS** MILES ☐ MINS. ☐ CALS. ☐ AVG. $\frac{CAL}{MIN}$ ☐	**WEEK # TOTALS** MILES ☐ MINS. ☐ CALS. ☐ AVG. $\frac{CAL}{MIN}$ ☐	**WEEK # TOTALS** MILES ☐ MINS. ☐ CALS. ☐ AVG. $\frac{CAL}{MIN}$ ☐	**FOUR WEEK TOTAL** MILES ☐ MINS. ☐ CALS. ☐ AVG. $\frac{CAL}{MIN}$ ☐

NEW GRAND TOTAL
MILES ☐
MINS. ☐
CALS. ☐
AVG. $\frac{CAL}{MIN}$ ☐

	START OF MONTH	**END OF MONTH**
BODY WEIGHT	—— pounds	—— pounds
BLOOD PRESS	———————	———————
RESTING PULSE	—— beats/min	—— beats/min
FITNESS LEVEL	1 2 3 4 5 6 7 8 9	1 2 3 4 5 6 7 8 9

**The back side of
this page is your**

TREADMILL TRAINING LOG

*Carefully slice this page out of your book; make
13 clear copies of it, and you're set with a full
year of scorecards for your treadmill training.*

Cut clearly
along this line.

TREADMILL TRAINING LOG CHART

	WEEK #	WEEK #	WEEK #	WEEK #
MON MILES				
MINS.				
CALS.				
TUE MILES				
MINS.				
CALS.				
WED MILES				
MINS.				
CALS.				
THU MILES				
MINS.				
CALS.				
FRI MILES				
MINS.				
CALS.				
SAT MILES				
MINS.				
CALS.				
SUN MILES				
MINS.				
CALS.				

WEEK # TOTALS	WEEK # TOTALS	WEEK # TOTALS	WEEK # TOTALS	FOUR WEEK TOTAL
MILES	MILES	MILES	MILES	MILES
MINS.	MINS.	MINS.	MINS.	MINS.
CALS.	CALS.	CALS.	CALS.	CALS.
AVG. CAL/MIN	AVG. CAL/MIN	AVG. CAL/MIN	AVG. CAL/MIN	AVG. CAL/MIN

YEAR TO DATE
MILES
MINS.
CALS.
AVG. CAL/MIN

NEW GRAND TOTAL
MILES
MINS.
CALS.
AVG. CAL/MIN

	START OF MONTH	END OF MONTH
BODY WEIGHT	____ pounds	____ pounds
BLOOD PRESS	_____	_____
RESTING PULSE	___ beats/min	___ beats/min
FITNESS LEVEL	1 2 3 4 5 6 7 8 9	1 2 3 4 5 6 7 8 9

Chapter 9

TEN QUESTIONS THAT CONFUSE TREADMILL WALKERS

Separating fact from fiction; throwing out the myths.

Question 1.   Is it better to train on a treadmill **fast** & **flat** (high speed @ low elevation) or **slow** & **steep** (low speed @ high elevation)?

Answer. Walking slowly on an incline can produce the same aerobic effect as walking much faster on level ground. For example, walking on a treadmill at 4.5 mph @ 0% grade yields about the same workload as walking 3.5 mph @ 10% grade. However, from a mechanical standpoint, the knees, hips and backs of most walkers will hold up better walking at a more reasonable cadence of 110 to 120 footsteps per minute (3.5 to 4.0 mph) than at 130 to 150 footsteps per minute. In a way it's like automobiles. Their engines run better and last longer at 3000 revolutions per minute (RPM's) as opposed to 6000 RPM's. The same holds true for your body and your treadmill. They'll both last longer "running at moderate RPM's."

Alternate Answer. A second argument can be made in favor of varying your routines such that you split your training between **slow-steep** and **fast-flat** workouts. This has a motivational advantage (more variety; less boredom); plus it causes different muscle groups to get exercised on a rotational basis. However, even if you're going to follow this strategy, it would be advantageous to vary your workouts between 5% and 15% grade as opposed to 0% and 10% grade.

Question 2. Which is better, **treadmill running** or **treadmill walking**?

Answer. In treadmill walking there is considerably less stress on your body (compared to running) since one foot is always grounded while walking. This translates to impact landing forces in walking which are one-half to one-third less than those of running. The simple solution then becomes raising the elevation on your treadmill. This permits you to hit your target heart rate without pounding the treadmill platform, and without jarring your bones and joints. And your heart will never know the difference – running, walking, swimming, whatever – as long as the exercise workload intensity is maintained.

Question 3. How does **regular walking** compare to **treadmill walking**?

Answer. For most people, treadmill walking is much more vigorous since there is no *sluffing off* (the belt moves — you move). Also, in treadmill walking, target heart rates can be sustained more easily because of the ability to work against gravity on long uphill stretches. This lets you burn more calories – in some cases twice as many calories. Lastly, footing is more consistent on a treadmill than on outdoor surfaces, minimizing ankle, knee, hip and back inflammations.

Question 4. How much time do you really need to spend per week on a Treadmill Walking Program?

Answer. A lot depends on your goals, but in general you can use the following rule of thumb: **one hour per week is good. Two hours per week is better. Three hours per week is best.** The Harvard Alumni study indicates that we can improve our longevity by increasing our physical activity to a minimum level of 2000 Calories per week. For the average sized person, three hours a week of treadmill walking can easily burn 1500 of those 2000 Calories!

Question 5. What's the **best time** of the day for a treadmill workout: morning, mid-day or evening?

Answer. Plain and simple, it does not matter – as long as you enjoy working out at that time. The time which suits you on a consistent basis is really the best time! Hence your work schedule, social commitments and family obligations will play a major part in blocking out your training times.

Question 6. Is it best to walk on a treadmill **before** or **after** eating?

Answer. If you're planning an intense workout, it is **not** advisable to walk directly after a meal. Wait one to two hours. However, easy-gaited walks directly following a meal can aid digestion, relieve that bloated, lazy feeling, and help you burn extra fat at elevated metabolism. A great way to lose weight is to take short strolls after every meal. Even three-minute treadmill walks help!

Question 7. How does a **motorized treadmill** compare to a **bicycle ergometer, rowing machine, stair climber** or **cross-country ski machine**?

Answer. Biking and rowing are not full weight-bearing exercises. Stationary bikes provide little upper body workout – plus the seats irritate many people after repeated use. Rowers are too strenuous on the upper body for many people, resulting in a high drop-out rate. Cross-Country Ski machines require too much motor coordination for the average person. Stair climbing can be tough on the Achilles tendon, and it's not as safe as walking on a wide-open treadmill platform. In summary, treadmills provide easy, safe, comfortable, and highly effective weight-bearing exercise – with minimal impact. Because treadmill walking is so natural, you can sustain the effort much longer and ultimately burn more calories.

Question 8. Is it better to walk **fast** for **short** durations, or to take **longer** workouts at a **moderate** pace?

Answer. For **cardiovascular conditioning**, high-intensity workouts of moderate duration are best. For **weight loss**, longer workouts (45 minutes and up) at a more moderate intensity will help you burn more fat. Using Trotter's 540 Supertrainer training system, anyone can customize his or her own mix of workouts to accomplish specific fitness goals as shown below:

THE 540 SUPERTRAINER WEEKLY SCHEDULE

TREADMILL PROGRAM	WEEKLY TRAINING	WORKOUT DURATION
Weight Loss Walking	Four P2 workouts One P3 workout One P5 workout	3.00 hours 0.50 hours 0.25 hours 3.75 hours
Cardiovascular Conditioning	Three P3 workouts Two P5 workouts	1.50 hours 0.50 hours 2.00 hours
Balanced Training	One P2 workout Two P3 workouts One P4 workout Two P5 workouts	0.75 hours 1.00 hour 0.50 hours 0.50 hours 2.75 hours
The 540 ST Protocols	P1 = Self-Evaluation program P2 = Weight Loss program P3 = Cardiovascular program P4 = Speed Interval program P5 = Maintenance program	

Question 9. Are hand-held weights worthwhile?

Answer. Yes, but not during a walk! Hand-weights distort your natural, free rhythm (ankle weights are even worse). They also add little to the overall metabolic effect. Remember also, that as your muscles strengthen to accomodate the hand-weights' resistance, the effect of these weights is lost. If you already own a set of hand-weights, use them as free-weights for muscle-toning exercises at times when you can slowly control the lifting motion.

Question 10. Is it necessary to work up a sweat on a treadmill?

Answer. No – but it helps! Sweating is the body's way of cooling off. It's a form of evaporative cooling. Other than a thermometer, sweat may be your best predictor of core temperature. When your core temperature is elevated, the mitochondria within your muscle cells are actively burning stored body fat at an accelerated rate. The adrenalin in your bloodstream and your elevated body temperature drive your metabolism. As the fat is burned, it is converted to water, heat and carbon dioxide – all of which are disposed as you exhale air and perspire. So if you sweat during your workouts, it's a good sign of elevated metabolism. Just remember to replace the lost fluids by drinking sufficient amounts of water.

However, if you're not comfortable working up a sweat, don't worry about it. You'll still burn calories, tone muscles and reduce stress. You'll even save on shower time, hot water and soap. The most important thing is to work out at an intensity level which you enjoy – sweat or no sweat!

Chapter 10

THE GLOSSARY OF TREADMILL TRAINING
Forty treadmill and fitness training terms worth knowing.

Adjusted Treadmill Workload (AW) A measure of one's workload taking into account both treadmill speed (mph) and elevation (% grade). Estimated by the formula: **AW = speed + (% grade) ÷ 10**. Example: 4 mph @ 8% grade yields an **AW** of 4.8 mph which translates to walking 4.8 mph @ 0% grade.

Aerobic   Occurring when the oxygen delivery system matches the oxygen demand of the active muscles.

Aerobic Target Zone   The recommended range of heart rate intensities for optimal training. Calculated as a percentage of one's maximum heart rate.

Aerobic Treadmilling   Treadmill exercise in which the muscles burn fat and sugar in the presence of sufficient oxygen supplies.

Anaerobic   Occuring when the oxygen demand of the active muscles exceeds the ability of the oxygen delivery system. As a result, large quantities of lactic acid are produced.

Anaerobic Threshold   The transition point at which an increasing workload forces muscles to burn fuel without sufficient supplies of oxygen.

Basal Metabolism   The minimum amount of calories burned by the body while sleeping. Usually expressed as 1 metabolic equivalent (1 MET).

Belt Tracking   The right to left positioning of the treadmill belt on its rollers. Correct tracking means the belt is centered over the platform board.

Blood Pressure   The pressure (force per unit area) exerted by circulating blood on the inside blood vessel walls.

Bradycardia   Any resting heart rate less than 60 beats per minute.

Cadence   The total number of right and left footsteps taken in a minute of walking. Typical range: 100 to 120 steps per minute.

calorie   The amount of energy it takes to raise 1 gram of water 1°C. Also known as a small calorie or a gram calorie.

Calorie   The amount of energy it takes to raise 1 kilogram of water 1°C.   Also known as a kilocalorie (kcal) or a large Calorie (equals 1000 small calories).

Cycle Mode   The operating mode on any treadmill in which the control panel automatically cycles through its critical parameters.

Heart Rate Recovery   The return to normal resting heart rate following exercise.

Heel-Toe Walking   The walker's natural foot motion – i.e. the walker's foot lands on the heel, rolls over the ball, and pushes off on the toes.

Inertial Flywheel   Directly coupled to the motor, this weight helps maintain momentum for smooth treadmill operation.

Kilometer   A unit of length equal to 0.62 miles.   Ten kilometers is 6.2 miles.

Maximum Attainable Heart Rate (MAHR)   The highest proven heart rate which an individual can achieve under stress.   Estimated by the formula: MAHR = 220 - One's Age.

Metabolism   The sum total rate of all chemical and enzyme reactions in the body as fats, oxygen and carbohydrates are converted to energy, heat, water and carbon dioxide.

MET   The average amount of oxygen used per 2.2 pounds (1Kg) of body weight in the resting state (basal metabolism).   One MET (for the average person) is 3.5 milliliters of oxygen per kilogram of body weight, which on the average, translates to an energy expenditure of one Calorie per minute.

Moving Recovery   A type of cool-down in which the body recovers to a lower metabolic state while in motion.

Newton's Law of Inertia   A body in motion tends to stay in motion; a body at rest tends to stay at rest (direct ramifications to "couch potatoes").

Overuse Syndrome   A training injury caused by excessive exercise repetitions. Cure: rest and slow rehabilitation.

Pace   One's walking or running speed measured by the time taken to cover a mile.

Percent Grade   The incline of a treadmill, calculated as a percentage of rise in elevation per unit of horizontal length (i.e. 10% grade is a 1 foot rise in elevation for every 10 feet of horizontal distance).

Post-Exercise Metabolism   The extra metabolic burn experienced directly after an exercise workout (can last several hours).

Pritikin Interval Workout   A 45-minute treadmill workout incorporating an alternating series of high and low intensity walks (or runs).

Pronation   An excessive inward rotation of the foot on landing, often occurring in people with flat feet.

Shin Splints   A painful muscle injury in the front leg region located about halfway between the knee and ankle resulting from either: (1) improper warm-up, (2) overuse, (3) muscle imbalance, or (4) wearing improper shoes.

Side Stitches   Sharp shooting pains between the ribs due to poor oxygen supply caused by insufficient warm-up and training too intensely.

Stride Length   The consistent distance measured between two consecutive foot-steps (i.e. left heel strike to right heel strike).

Training Effect   The sum of all physiological improvements including: (1) increased heart stroke volume; (2) improved oxygen uptake; (3) reduction in body fat; and (4) lower resting and exercise heart rates.

Treadmill Belt   A continuous mat – several feet wide – which tracks on rollers to provide a smooth walking surface.

Treadmill Cool-down   A short period of easy-gaited walking following a workout; enables the body to gradually re-adjust to a resting state.

Treadmill Display   The treadmill control panel containing the STOP, START, SPEED and ELEVATION switches, digital readouts and computer controls.

Treadmill Interval Training   A method of training using alternating intervals of high- and low-intensity aerobic work.

Treadmill Program Profile   The actual interval-by-interval changes in % grade and speed comprising the total workout.

Treadmill Shoulder   Foot pads located on both sides of the treadmill to help the user safely step on and off the treadmill.

Treadmill Warm-up   A short period of easy-gaited walking preceding a workout; enables the body to make a transition from the resting state to a higher-metabolic aerobic state.

For **technical information** on Treadmill Walking, direct your questions to: Rob Sweetgall, Creative Walking Inc., P.O. Box 699, Newark, DE 19711 or call 302-368-2222.

For **product information** concerning treadmills write to Trotter, 1073 Main Street, Millis, MA 02054 or call 1-800-227-1632.

PERSONAL TREADMILL NOTES